PHAR LAP

Geoff Armstrong's passion for racing dates back to the early 1960s, when his grandfather taught him to read using a Saturday form guide while recounting tales of Phar Lap and other champions of the turf. Armstrong is the author of *Century of Summers*, the centenary book of the Sheffield Shield, and ESPN's *Legends of Cricket*, a study of the game's 25 greatest players. He compiled and edited the first ever anthology of Australian rugby league, *The Greatest Game*, and is the co-author of a number of sports books, including *The People's Game*, a history of Australia in international one-day cricket, *Whiticisms* (1995), with Mike Whitney, *Winning Attitudes*, an analysis of prominent Australian athletes produced especially for the Sydney Olympics, *Hands & Heals*, the autobiography of Ian Healy, and *The Best of Bevan* with Michael Bevan. Armstrong has also worked with Steve Waugh on each of Waugh's 10 best-selling books.

Peter Thompson's fascination with racing began when his grandmother backed Piping Lane at 40–1 to win the 1972 Melbourne Cup. As a commentator on sporting issues, his opini⟨ read in the *Age*, *The Financial Review* and BRW and he⟨ Thommo from the Track on Melbourne Radio's 3AW. ⟨ several slow horses, he has often been heard to invok⟨ the hopelessly optimistic: 'Even Phar Lap ran last in ⟨

PHAR LAP

HOW A HORSE BECAME A HERO OF HIS TIME
AND AN ICON OF A NATION

GEOFF ARMSTRONG
PETER THOMPSON

A Sue Hines Book
Allen & Unwin

First published in hardback in 2000
This revised edition published in 2003

A Sue Hines Book
Allen & Unwin
83 Alexander Street
Crows Nest NSW 2065
Australia
Phone: (61 2) 8425 0100
Fax: (61 2) 9906 2218
Email: info@allenandunwin.com
Web: www.allenandunwin.com

National Library of Australia
Cataloguing-in-Publication entry:
Armstrong, Geoff.
Phar Lap.
Rev. ed.
ISBN 1 86508 994 X (pbk.).
1. Phar Lap (Race horse). 2. Race horses – Australia. 3. Horse racing –
Australia. I. Thompson, Peter, 1960– . II. Title.
798.400994

Photograph on p.165: Phar Lap training at Agua Caliente,
source Museum Victoria

Text design by Studio Pazzo
Typeset by Pauline Haas
Printed by McPherson's Printing Group

10 9 8 7 6 5 4 3 2 1

Contents

Prologue

5 APRIL 1932

It was a little more than a fortnight since Phar Lap had won the rich Agua Caliente Handicap in Mexico. He was recovering well from a minor operation on his injured hoof and now, in the palatial surrounds of the Menlo Park property just south of San Francisco, the Australian champion's small travelling party was beginning to relax. The tension of their trip from the other side of the world, and the preparation for a race over ten furlongs among the silent watchers, the thieves and the shadows of the casino town, had dissipated. A movie deal was to be signed that day. Hundreds of people were visiting the stables each afternoon to see the wonderhorse.

As Tommy Woodcock, the horse's former strapper and now trainer, rose at his usual hour of 4.30 a.m. on 5 April 1932, he was looking forward to continuing the program of light work he had plotted for the gelding the US media was admitting could be the best racehorse in the world. He had slept the night in the stall opposite the champion's. As soon as Tommy was out of bed, he crossed to Phar Lap's stall and offered his closest friend a morning sugar cube. For the first time in the two and a half years that the pair had been inseparable, Phar Lap was uninterested in the ritual gift. 'Bobby's breath was hot and he was steaming under his rug,' Woodcock recalled later.

Bill Nielsen, the Australian vet travelling with Phar Lap, was quickly summoned. Phar Lap's pulse was irregular and his temperature slightly elevated. Nielsen's diagnosis was colic, an intestinal malady not uncommon in horses, but occasionally fatal. Standard treatment for colic was a drench, and one was administered immediately by Nielsen and Woodcock. They were both confident Bobby would make a quick recovery.

After an initial improvement, by 11.30 a.m. Phar Lap's condition had deteriorated. His temperature was 102°F and Nielsen was gravely concerned. He ordered Woodcock to keep Phar Lap walking in the yard and dashed off to seek the assistance of Dr Masoero, the vet at the nearby Tanforan racecourse.

As Tommy Woodcock walked his beloved companion around the yard, he was overwhelmed by Phar Lap's suffering. The gelding's stomach was bloated and he was retching and groaning with pain. Time was the only possible cure. He had to be kept upright and moving for long enough to allow the medication to work, and for two hours Woodcock dragged his brave horse around the yard. Tough as he was, the pain finally became too much. Woodcock saw the light go from the champion's eyes. Gone were the days when Phar Lap would take Woodcock for a walk through the streets, with Tommy calling 'Bobby, Bobby', trying to make his mate slow down. It was over. Tommy led Phar Lap to his stall, where he fell to the floor.

Just after 2 p.m. Phar Lap lifted his head, nuzzled Tommy under the arm, spurted bloody fluid from his nostrils, and died.

Cashy's champion

On 6 April 1932, the Prime Minister of Australia, Joseph Lyons, was in a very happy and contented mood. He had just learned that the High Court had backed a crucial piece of legislation, on which he had staked his reputation. It seemed, too, generally speaking, that the worst of the Great Depression was behind the country, though he was fully aware there was still so much to be done. He straightened his tie and was searching for his hat, when one of his staff rushed towards him. More cabled news, sir, but of a different, dreadful kind: the horse, Phar Lap, has died in California.

Joe Lyons was not a racing man, but he knew Phar Lap and the impact that the champion racehorse had made on the community, how much the nation had revered his Melbourne Cup win and celebrated his recent triumph in America. He needed to make a brief comment and wanted to get it right. A crowd of reporters was gathered outside, and soon after the Prime Minister was respectfully telling them, 'What is the use of winning a High Court decision and losing Phar Lap? The death of this wonderful horse is a great sporting tragedy.'

HOW MANY PEOPLE, three years before that awful day, could possibly have predicted that the death of this horse called Phar Lap would capture the attention of racing fans on both sides of the Pacific and sadden even the Australian Prime Minister? In February 1929, Phar Lap was a scraggy, unraced two-year-old, who had been purchased at a yearling sale in New Zealand the previous summer for just 160 guineas on a day when a more glamorous colt had sold for 2300 guineas, a New Zealand record. His trainer was going so badly that none of his diminishing list of regular clients had accepted his advice to purchase the horse. On taking one look at him, the man who did put the money up to buy him refused to accept him, finally swinging a deal with the trainer that would best cut his losses. The man who would become his faithful attendant devoted as much time to the immature gelding as he could, but out of necessity sought other more lucrative jobs as well.

The only bloke who thought Phar Lap would be a champion from day one was a boy, all of fifteen years and 1.5 metres tall, called Heaton Cashell Martin—'Cashy' or 'Cash' to his mates, of whom there were plenty. A bright little fella with a rascal's grin and a character to match, in early 1929 he lived with his mother, a single parent, his two sisters and a brother in a little house at 17 Bowral St, Kensington, a working-class suburb around 10 kilometres south of Sydney's city centre, and just a very short gallop away from its most famous racecourse, at Randwick. They made ends meet, just. Cashy was one of those little terriers everyone looked forward to seeing again. He'd been drawn to the track from before he could remember, and now, still looking every bit as new and breakable as he was, he sat well on a horse and might have a future. He took a shine to the ugly, leggy chestnut called Phar Lap (a Thai word, pharlap, means 'emitting light from the sky'—an appropriate name for a progeny of Night Raid) from the first time he met him, not too long after the day, Cashy's fourteenth birthday, when he became a fully fledged apprentice with Mr Telford, the trainer whose stables were as good as next door to home. Of course, to care for such a horse was a huge responsibility for an inexperienced lad, but Telford was so short of ready cash that it was all the trainer could do. Telford, when he could afford to, co-opted a couple of young strappers, Tom Sumner and Aaron Treve 'Tommy' Woodcock, to help out. And he devoted a great deal of time to the task himself. Otherwise, Cashy or the other stable apprentice, the slightly older Arthur Percy, had the job.

As any impressionable lad was prone to do, Cashy assumed his horse was going to be a champion. You could tell by the look in Phar Lap's eye, even if everyone else told him that the gelding looked more like a cross between a small giraffe and a giant kangaroo than a race-horse. The fact that the boss would sometimes pat the horse and say 'He might be o'right this bloke' did nothing to dampen Cashy's confidence. If the local schoolkids were hanging round the stables, as they often did, and Cashy was in charge, which sometimes happened, he'd offer them a ride. 'Anyone wanna ride a Melbourne Cup winner?' he'd grin, and one or two would accept the opportunity of a lifetime. But this would only happen if Mr Telford or Mr Woodcock or Mr Sumner weren't about.

ON 22 FEBRUARY 1929, Cashy Martin was scampering home and snatching glances at his newspaper, the tabloid of the day, the Daily Pictorial, as he ran. On the racing page, listing the fields for tomorrow at Rosehill, the Pictorial named 'A. Perry' as the jockey. But that was wrong. The jockey was going be 'Apprentice H. Martin, claiming seven'. Cashy had jumped out of bed even earlier than usual that Friday morning to, as it turned out, squander a precious penny on the paper. He'd wanted to show his mum and his mates that his name was next to his horse. Instead they'd put 'A. Perry'! They couldn't even spell it right, for 'A. Perry', he assumed, meant Arthur Percy. Cashy's mum said it didn't matter—'They make mistakes all the time!'—but it did. Still, what could you do but prove them wrong. Not to worry, he laughed to his mum as he headed again for the door, maybe it'll help the price. Down the steps he went and out into the 'Kenso' morning, chuckling to himself as he imagined the big punters in the betting ring changing their minds because he was in the saddle. They would for Mr Pike, maybe one day for me . . .

Cashy flicked through the headlines, bustling along as he did, stopping to read only what interested him. Something 'bout the new bridge—maybe what decade it's gonna be finished in! And, loud across the sports pages, another story of the new young batting stars, Bradman and Jackson, scoring hundreds against the Poms. Jackson was as good as Victor Trumper, so a bloke at the stables had said, and Trumper, so he reckoned, was the best there ever was. Back to page three, where the paper reported grimly on the feared razor gangs: about an attack in the city, on the corner of Castlereagh and Campbell, which had left a pretty young girl in hospital and another punk in the lock-up. At six o'clock last night! In the middle of town! There was talk of the king of the skies, Kingsford Smith, and strikes and stock exchanges, but Cashy's eyes went back to the racing pages, to stories of the wonder-colt Strephon, the old champ Amounis, the Kiwi Limerick and the mighty Mollison, favourite for the Newmarket. Cashy searched for any mention of the jockeys—his idols—Jim Munro, brother of his good mate Darby, and Jim Pike. And the Melbourne ace, Billy Duncan, and the veteran, Bobby Lewis, who'd won a Cup on Trivalve in '27, and three other Cups, too.

Mr Telford was a tough boss, as tough on his horses and jockeys as life currently was on him. Born in Ballarat, Victoria, fifty-two years earlier, but raised in New Zealand, he had made his reputation as the stable foreman for Richard Mason, trainer of, among others, the legendary Gloaming, star of the Randwick carnivals of the early twenties. Mr Telford had settled in Sydney with dreams of finding his own Gloaming, but things hadn't worked out yet. And probably never would. Pundits described him as a 'battling' trainer, but 'broke' would have been closer. Year after year Telford bought well-bred but inexpensive yearlings from New Zealand—he was well-versed in bloodlines and reckoned he knew what would work—but year after bloody year they proved to be not very good or no good at all. He craved a reasonable horse, so he could regularly pay the rent and the track managers, and also look after his wife and young son, and get a full-time foreman rather than scrounging the services of anyone who happened to be available on a day-by-day basis. Now, in the summer of 1928–29, most of his owners had gone. Cashy knew things were tricky: more than once he'd seen his mum and Mr Telford lookin' more than serious. He'd noticed, too, that Mr Woodcock and Mr Sumner were doing more work for other stables. 'Man can't work for nothin', Cash,' Mr Woodcock would say.

But Mr Woodcock would be okay. Next to Mr Telford, no-one knew more about horses than Mr Woodcock. He'd taught Cashy so much already—about when to be tough with a horse, when to be gentle, how they 'talked' and why they looked you in the eye. Mr Woodcock was as kind with horses as Mr Telford was tough. Their hearts were in the same place, Cashy knew that, but their methods were far apart. It struck Cashy that they would not last together for long. Unless, of course, Phar Lap kept them together, for Mr Woodcock had fallen for the horse too. He, like Mr Telford, called the young horse by his nickname, 'Bobby', a habit Cashy also enjoyed. The young lad dreamed of the day, not too distant, when they'd break through, win a big race: Mr Telford in the mounting yard chatting with the owners, Mr Woodcock bringing the horse in,

Cashy wearing the stable colours—red, black-and-white hooped sleeves, red cap—Mr Telford giving the instructions, Mr Woodcock lifting him into the saddle, Cashy going out onto the track ...

Back to reality. Paper read, Cashy started thinking again about tomorrow. Nobody reckons he can win, 'cept me. Not even Mr Woodcock. 'Cash, 'e's just in for the learnin',' was what he said. But Cashy'd show 'em. The smile couldn't leave his face. ''E's gonna be a champ, is our 'orse,' Cashy grinned to anyone who saw him. 'Even the boss thinks 'e's gonna be a champ!'

Though Harry Telford hadn't said as much. A short, weatherbeaten, some said sour man, with his dark, greying hair slicked tight beneath his felt hat or cap, it wasn't his style to say as much. Cashy knew that. The trainer's greatest loyalty was to his wife and young son, then to those who worked hard for him, or stuck loyal to him. Never tell 'em—meaning 'outsiders'—what they don't need to know, son, the trainer had reminded the apprentice. To Harry Telford, educating young horsemen wasn't just about teaching them how to sit. Be cautious, trust no-one, be your own man. Be careful. Harry Telford didn't encourage Cashy Martin because of his rascal's cheek or his grin; he liked what he saw in the boy's dedication, his capacity to learn, his street-smarts. And the way his ragged clothes were always as neat as they could be.

Cashy was carefully optimistic. If I win on 'im tomorrow, they'll never get me off ... 'And there goes, Phar Lap, three, four, five lengths clear, Martin ridin' for dear life,' Cashy yelled into his fist, aping the racecallers. 'Cup's over, ladies and gentleman. Look at 'im go! He's another Carbine, is this Phar Lap! ... Better than Carbine!!'

'And what a ride by little Cash Martin, his first Melbourne Cup winner ...'

Like Cashy's home, Telford's stables were in Bowral Street, right opposite where the legendary trainer Tommy Smith later established his world-famous Tulloch Lodge. Telford's set-up was simply four old boxes and a sand yard, around which Cashy often walked Phar Lap for hours at a time. This was where he would parade the gelding for the benefit of his army of young friends on their way to or from the local school, which was on the corner of Bowral Street and Doncaster Avenue, right opposite the course. What Cashy didn't tell them was that he wasn't allowed to take Phar Lap out onto the street, for once the fractious two-year-old got a taste of freedom, he was way too strong for the boy.

Jim Marsh (later a rails bookmaker in Sydney): He wasn't a pretty horse. Phar Lap as a two-year-old was like a bloke who's about six foot six. A big, raw, awkward bastard, with arms everywhere, and a long ugly neck. You could see the muscles, if you looked for them, but they didn't show out when he was just standing. But, gee, he was strong; you could see how strong he was when he marched along. Even then, his legs seemed too big for his body ...

Woodcock was the only one who could handle the horse. They used to walk around the streets of Kensington, but Tommy didn't take Phar Lap for a walk—Phar Lap took Tommy for a walk. Often times, it seemed he was going to get away from Woodcock, but Woodcock could talk to him.

All you'd hear, walking down Milroy Avenue and Todman Avenue and places like that, was Woodcock yelling, 'Bobby! Bobby! Bobby!' We thought the coppers were coming.

ON THAT FRIDAY before Phar Lap's race debut, Cashy was off to see his mates, of whom eleven-year-old Jim Marsh was one, to let them know what was happening. Jim was one of the privileged few to have ridden the two-year-old around the sand yard. 'Our horse, Bobby,' he hollered when he found them, 'the one that's gonna win the Cup. Fellas, he's in tomorrow, at the 'hill, and I'm on 'im.'

'Is he gonna win, Cashy?'

'Course he's gonna win. Get's a tarp, will ya, we're 'aving a muster!'

'Is he really gonna win?'

''Ave I ever lied to you?'

Conversation stopped for a moment. 'Give us that tarp, will ya,' Cashy was a little flustered. A muster was a 'tarpaulin muster'—only to be called when a horse was a good thing. Money was precious for these young fellas. One of them grabbed a bit of old canvas, spread it on the ground. Someone quickly threw in a sixpence. No poker faces here. Another, rich bastard, had a shilling. Next a halfpenny. All up, it didn't amount to much, about eight quid, just a small fortune. 'With that sort of money,' Jim Marsh chuckled when recalling the event seventy years later, 'we could've nearly bought the horse.' Cashy threw in more than he had. 'Better than bank interest, I reckon,' he laughed.

Whatever bank interest was . . .

THE NEXT DAY Phar Lap ran a shocker, at 33–1, in the first division of the Rosehill Race Club's Nursery Handicap over five and a half furlongs. The race was won by the favourite, Exact, from Cabaret Girl and Pimento. Most of the papers missed Phar Lap completely. The Sydney Morning Herald listed the first five across the line, and 'Phar Lap last'. Telford wasn't concerned: for him the race was part of an education process, never cause for a muster or a chase for a cheque. The young horse proved a real handful for his rookie rider, missing the jump, fighting the bridle and refusing to run true when asked for a sprint up the straight. In the end, it was all Cashy could do to get him over the line in one piece. There'd be another day . . .

The Breeding

The colt that became Phar Lap was purchased at the Trentham Thoroughbred Yearling Sales on 24 January 1928 for the miserly sum of 160 guineas. Harry Telford had spotted Lot 41, a colt by the poorly performed Night Raid from the broken-down New Zealand mare Entreaty, in the sales catalogue and was impressed by its breeding. How could the youngster that was to become the greatest racehorse of its time, and arguably the best of all time, be knocked down so cheaply?

The *Bloodstock Breeders' Review* of 1929, published in the United Kingdom, described the early life of Phar Lap's sire:

Night Raid, the sire of Phar Lap, was bred in England by Major F.C. Stern in 1918, but was so little fancied as a yearling that Mr Douglas-Pennant bought him for only 160 guineas. In England, it ran 6 times for Mr A Douglas-Pennant and was placed third twice—in the Dunstall 2 year-old Selling Plate at Wolverhampton on 25th May 1920 and the Juvenile Selling Plate at Salisbury on 7th July. At the end of his two-year-old season was again submitted to auction and Mr P. Keith, of Sydney, became his owner for 120 guineas. Night Raid was put into training in Sydney, and won one race for Mr Keith, who then sold him to Mr A. P. Wade, who won half a race (dead heat for first) with him. The horse broke down while on a visit to Melbourne, and Mr Wade disposed of him for a few hundred guineas to Mr A. F. Roberts, owner of a small stud at Timaru, New Zealand.

In 1925, Night Raid served a mare called Entreaty and on 4 October 1926 she foaled a chestnut colt with white hind pasterns and a small half moon blaze. There was something in that colt's pedigree that caught Telford's eye, but was missed by everyone else.

We don't know what it was that made him want that horse. He could not have possibly known if it was powered by a rocket or a rubber band. But Telford must have appreciated that the probabilities presented by Phar Lap's five-generation pedigree improved the chances of the colt turning into a handy horse. He did not have enough money to buy the horse himself, but thought well enough of the breeding to try to persuade one of his dwindling band of clients to buy the horse unseen.

In Ballarat, where Telford was born, his father had owned a livery stable, and had occasionally trained thoroughbreds. At one stage Telford senior trained a gelding called Nimblefoot for a local publican, Walter Craig. Although poorly performed (to the extent that the handicapper allocated it six stone for the 1870 Melbourne Cup), Craig persisted with the horse and sent it to prominent Flemington trainer, W. Lang, for its Cup campaign. Some months before the Cup, Craig dreamt that a horse carrying his racing colours won the Cup, but with the jockey wearing a black armband. He told the story to a number of friends and died the following night. Nimblefoot duly won the Cup, with a black crepe band tied to the jockey's arm. Harry Telford's father boasted often to his young sons that he had trained a Melbourne Cup winner.

In a later interview with the Melbourne *Herald*, Telford related exactly how he came to be Phar Lap's trainer.

My father having been a trainer, I was reared among horses. From early boyhood pedigrees interested me. I have studied thousands and thousands of them. When the catalogue of the sale at which Phar Lap was offered reached me, I ran through it in the usual way. Phar Lap's breeding caught my eye. The more I went into it the stronger grew my belief that here was a perfectly bred animal—just the sort of horse I had been hoping to train.

I spent more than a month, sitting up night after night, studying Phar Lap's pedigree. I was sure I had found a winner, but I was afraid to say too much in case someone else might get in before me.

I knew that Mr Davis was a buyer of horses, so I suggested that he should buy the youngster. Mr Davis said he had enough horses already. When I explained the exceptional breeding of this one, he asked me what he was like in the legs. He wasn't at all keen, and for a long time I could not get him to make up his mind.

I thought I would try someone else, and I actually went out to Moorefield races one day to do that. On the course I met Mr Davis and for the last time pressed him to buy. He said he would if the horse was sound, so I said to him, 'I'll see to that; you get someone to bid for you.'

David J. Davis, a dumpy American-born self-promoter and businessman, knowing Telford's reputation as a judge of racehorses, had once asked his advice about purchasing one of a draft of English mares. Telford recommended Time-Will-Tell, which proved to be untrainable. Despite this initial misadventure, Telford eventually targeted Davis as the financier of Lot 41.

This must have been a risk for the struggling trainer. Like most of his colleagues, Telford was keen to get a good horse owned by a rich man who paid his training bills. If Telford's judgement was good, he would collect winning percentages and might attract more horses to his stable. If the purchase was ill-founded, he risked alienating a client who was unlikely to return. Telford, clearly, could not afford to mislead Davis again.

Given the poor luck he had been experiencing, in all likelihood he did not have many alternatives. First stop had certainly been to Bob Price, a bookmaker and the one bloke who'd stuck solid through these tough times, to the point of coming good with loans when they were needed. At that time, Price owned the one promising horse in Telford's stable, a two-year-old filly called Eillom, but for the Night Raid colt he couldn't be cajoled. How Bob Price must have felt during the next three years, as he watched a money machine that could have been his, especially when Eillom became Phar Lap's best equine friend, to the point that Telford took her on trips to Melbourne and Adelaide ... to keep Phar Lap company.

AT THE SAME TIME in early 1928 that Harry Telford contacted his brother Hugh to ask him to check on the colt's soundness, David Davis wrote to Jack Sullings, a former employee based in Wellington. Davis asked Sullings—in a way which, if things had turned out differently, would have seemed arrogantly negligent—to bid for the horse. Davis was clearly half-hearted about the colt, suggesting that if he could not find anything better to do he might go to Trentham and bid no more than 200 guineas for Lot 41. Underwhelmed by the colt's looks, the market left Lot 41 to Jack Sullings and Hugh Telford for 160 guineas. Bidding completed, Sullings went on his way and Telford headed for the local shipping office, to get the colt on a boat for Sydney.

Tommy Woodcock, talking later with Jan Wositzky, recalled the scene when Davis came to inspect his new purchase.

The day that Phar Lap come, Mr Davis, the man that bought him for Mr Telford, he stood at the door and looked over the door. He never said a word for a while, and then in a nice quiet voice he said, 'Harry, I don't like the horse.' He said, 'I can't see my way clear for you training him for me.'

And Mr Telford looked and thought. 'Davis,' he said, 'I'm broke. I haven't got 160 guineas, or his fare over from New Zealand.'

Davis said, 'I don't care.'

And Telford thought for a while, and he said, ''I'll lease him off you.'

And Davis says, 'Yes, I'll lease him to you ... for three years.'

And Telford said, 'All right, thank you, that'll do.'

This proved to be the most lucrative business deal of Harry Telford's life.

However, there was a humiliation at the end of the negotiation that nettled Telford, a proud racing man. He had managed through the pain of having Davis tell him his judgement and the colt were no good. Finally, timidly, Telford asked that a clause be added to the lease, giving the trainer the right to claim a half share in the horse for £500. Right at that moment, even after he'd talked the horse so far up, the idea of Telford having a spare 500 quid over the next few years seemed fanciful. He knew that. But he didn't need this loud-mouthed Yank hollering, 'Harry, 500 to you would be worth 5000 to me! I don't think we'll worry about that.' And with that, David Davis clicked his heels and shuffled out of the stables.

I don't think he'll stay

Visitors to the Telford stables in the months leading up to Phar Lap's first race start had reckoned Phar Lap looked more like a scratchy, ragged 'kangaroo dog' than a thoroughbred racehorse. He was lazy, almost stolid, far from explosive. Telford remembered back to when Richard Mason had first seen Gloaming as a young colt. Many experts contended that the yearling was not robust enough to be a racehorse, but Mason believed that provided he was gelded he'd have a future. Indeed he did, for from 67 starts in New Zealand and Australia Gloaming recorded 57 wins and nine seconds (the one unplaced effort came when he got entangled in the starting rope and took no part!). Not surprisingly then, Harry Telford knew from day one that with his large frame his Night Raid colt would have more of a racing future as a gelding.

C.J. Graves (then one of Sydney's leading racing writers): From the very start, he [Phar Lap] showed the greatest unconcern for all the ills that beset a thoroughbred. Veterinary surgeon T.G. Doyle, who performed the operation that made him a gelding, was staggered at the physical resistance of the horse, even as a youngster. The operation over, Phar Lap pulled away to a patch of grass nearby and commenced unconcernedly picking. 'Put a saddle on him and you can ride him home,' said the vet to the attendant. 'That one doesn't need any nursing.'

After spelling through the winter of 1928 on a farm at Windsor, north-west of Sydney, Phar Lap had returned to Bowral Street as a two-year-old. The young horse and his trainer headed for the sandhills west of Kensington, near where the toffs played on their private golf courses, Telford telling bemused associates that he was going to toughen the horse up. More likely, some reckoned, he was dodging the shilling charged for working the horses at the track. Woodcock, from the day he found the two-year-old distressed and exhausted in his stall after another gruelling workout, deplored the way Telford poured the furlongs into his charge. 'Sudden death' Woodcock called it—Mr Telford would either make the gelding a racehorse or destroy him. Phar Lap quickly appreciated Woodcock's care, while the young horseman saw a magic in the gelding he'd never encountered in an animal before. Telford, to his eternal credit, quickly recognised the rapport between the two and encouraged as best he could a partnership that would become as famous as any in Australian sport.

Telford saw potential in the horse's big frame and toughened legs, and by the time of Phar Lap's raceday debut, was convinced he had a top-liner, if only his luck would hold. Maybe even a Derby horse. Woodcock, too, saw a bright future, while Cashy Martin recognised a power in the two-year-old's engine that was missing in the other stragglers he rode in trackwork and walked around the yard.

One racing man Telford did confide in was the great jockey Jim Pike. Back in 1922, Telford had booked Pike to ride his promising galloper, Solfanello, in the rich Doncaster Handicap, but after receiving negative reports about Pike's integrity, the horse's owners made Telford break the commitment. This he hated doing, especially as he knew the allegations to be bunkum. 'I trust you, Jim,' Telford told the jockey. 'And I hate the whole business. If I ever get another good'un, I hope you'll find a way to ride him for me.'

Pike understood. In 1936, he said of Telford, 'When you get to know him, a fine fellow who would walk over broken glass for you.' So when, in mid-1929, Harry Telford approached Pike at the races and quietly asked, 'Jim, please don't take another ride in the Derby yet,' Pike listened, even though he wasn't even sure, at this point, who this Phar Lap was.

A.B. Gray (veteran clocker at Randwick): Early in his two-year-old career, one took little notice of the chestnut as he was worked along in daylight by Harry Telford. But Harry, an astute trainer with years of experience, knew that he had something out of the ordinary.

One morning, just before Phar Lap won his first race, Bill Tindall saw him go so well that he said to Telford, 'Look here, Harry, I'll give you every horse in my stable, all fifteen of them, for Phar Lap.'

But Harry looked the other way.

'Battling Billy' Tindall was a crafty operator, big punter, and soon to be outed for twelve months when a punting sting went wrong. In the betting rings of Sydney and Melbourne, he was famous or notorious, depending on where your sympathies lay. In the Sydney *Truth*'s Sunday racing reports, his substantial wagers, and those of his big-punting cohorts, Rufe Naylor, Eric Connolly and the mysterious 'Madame X', Maude Vandenburg, consistently made headlines.

ON 2 MARCH 1929, Eric Connolly was in Melbourne, masterminding a massive and successful plunge on St Ardent in the big sprint at

Flemington, the Newmarket Handicap. The performance of Phar Lap, finishing a moderate seventh in a poor five-furlongs two-year-old handicap at the Sydney provincial track at Hawkesbury on the same day, would not have concerned the flamboyant 'Conn' at all. At Hawkesbury, Telford had promised the ride to Arthur Percy, in what would have been Arthur's first ride in a race. However, on race day, after studying the weak field and deciding Phar Lap had a genuine chance, the trainer turned to an older, more experienced apprentice, Frank Douglas. Later one of Melbourne's best jumps jockeys, young Douglas was reasonably impressed with Phar Lap, and whispered later to his master, Jack Phoenix, 'Well placed, he'll win races.'

Telford's wager at Hawkesbury was very small, and he would not reveal to the racing world anything of his Phar Lap hand until 1 April, Sydney Cup Day at Randwick. Phar Lap had finished well back again, in a six-furlongs two-year-old handicap at Rosehill on 16 March, but on that Cup day Telford entered his gelding in the Easter Stakes, against many of the best two-year-olds in training. Trainers of a number of horses that had beaten Phar Lap in his three runs to date, including the placegetters in his second and third starts, preferred the weaker Wentworth Handicap on the same card, but Harry Telford clearly believed he had a promising horse and wanted to test him against superior company.

He gave the ride to the tough seventeen-year-old apprentice Jack Baker, and instructed him to ride Phar Lap up near the lead. This Baker did, and the gelding stuck at it until well up the demanding Randwick straight, only capitulating in the final furlong, to finish eighth of eleven. The race was won by the statuesque colt Carradale, trained by the master, James Scobie, winner of four Melbourne Cups and countless Derbies, and owned by the chairman of the Victoria Racing Club, Mr L.K.S. (Lachlan) Mackinnon. Carradale had been purchased for 2000 guineas in New Zealand at around the same time

Phar Lap was being knocked down for 160. After the Easter Stakes, Mr Mackinnon, as wealthy as they come, was probably thinking how clever he was. So too, perhaps, was Harry Telford. A measuring stick for the improvement in his horse was the effort of Exact, the impressive winner of Phar Lap's first race start five weeks before, but this time an outclassed and well-beaten last.

HOWEVER PROMISE ALONE was not paying the rent. Woodcock continued to solicit work from other trainers, trying his darnedest to make sure it never impinged on his devotion to Telford's two-year-old. Cashy Martin was always available to ride the horse in work, even though he had lost the raceday rides to stronger, more experienced jockeys. Cashy still believed, still assured his mates at 'Kenso' that they'd get their tarp money back.

Harry Telford needed more than tarp money. And now, maybe, he had the answer. His horse had demonstrated in the Easter Stakes that, just as Telford had thought, he might be better than average. Yet he had finished no better than seventh in any of his four starts, and that was at Hawkesbury. But that meant that if he found the right race for the horse he'd probably get a price. Get a good price, and the debtors might stop knocking at the door. All in one shot. But he would be betting with money he did not have. Telford knew all about certainties in racing. There were none. Harry Telford had plenty of experience in betting stings, but after the knocks of recent years he had no faith in his ability to pull one off. But he had to.

Just as he'd scoured the sales catalogues more than a year before, now Telford scoured the racing calendar, searching for the right race, at the same time wondering where other trainers would place their horses. For three weeks, too cautious, he couldn't find what he wanted. He needed a race with pace in it, but also with at least a couple of reasonable contenders to ensure he got good odds. Finally, he settled on a maiden handicap at Rosehill on the last Saturday in April. A filly called Pure Tea, who'd finished second at Hawkesbury in Phar Lap's second start and since run fourth in a better class stakes race at Randwick, seemed the likely favourite. She was a front-runner, too, but in Telford's opinion a risk at the six furlongs. The Australian Jockey Club chairman, Mr Colin Stephen, had a starter, Voleuse, and Mr Stephen liked a bet. To disguise the fact that he'd earmarked the race, Telford entered his mare Eillom for the race immediately before the two-year-old event (she would run second, at 14–1). It was just another day at the races for Telford's team.

Leading Sydney racing writer Bill Whittaker, a noted expert and enthusiast on Phar Lap's life and racing career, believes that, to put the bets on, Telford turned to Jack Baker's master, Richard 'Dick' Wootton, a colourful veteran owner-trainer known on three continents for his shrewd betting and vast racing knowledge. Wootton had used the results of a successful plunge on his mare, Queen of Sheba, in the 1902 Metropolitan Handicap at Randwick to take off and see the world—first stop South Africa, then England—before heading back to Australia to become patriarch of one of Australian racing's most famous families. Dick Wootton's elder son, Frank, became one of England's leading jockeys, his younger son, Stanley, one of England's wealthiest owner-trainers and one of racing's most significant breeders.

Dick Wootton was an associate of Mr Theo Marks, a tall gentleman who, unlike some of his punting colleagues, kept a relatively low profile even though he wagered in substantial numbers. While Connolly, Naylor and company were referred to by name whenever their bets made the Truth's headlines, Marks was 'The Long 'Un', to less-informed readers a mysterious figure who might have worn a cape and mask. In reality, he was very much a part of the Sydney establishment, one of Sydney's leading architects and businessmen, and chairman of the Rosehill Race Club. One of Rosehill's leading races, the Theo Marks Quality Handicap, first run in 1946, remains today one of most important lead-up races to the AJC's Group One Epsom Handicap.

Wootton guaranteed Harry Telford he would get him the best price, which he shrewdly and patiently did. Theo Marks was obliged to wait for Wootton to complete his task, but would still get the opportunity to profit considerably as well. What would he have thought though when as soon as the bookies called 'Pure Tea, 3–1' punters stepped in and knocked the odds down to 2s? He was clearly not the only punter with good information. A bet of £600 to £200 Pure Tea was recorded, then £500 to £200, then £450 to £200, then £1000 to £500, £400 to £200, £200 to £100. Phar Lap was 10–1, 12–1, out to 15s. Cash came for a filly called Rose Flight, then in stepped the AJC Chairman's money. Mr Stephen's young trainer, Bayly Payten, had told his boss that Voleuse would 'give the others a thrashing', and quickly the leader of the ring, Jim Hackett, had written two bets of £600 to £100, then £250 to £50. Finally, 'right at the death,' *Truth* reported, 'the Long 'Un went round the ring and backed Phar Lap for big money.' Just before, Dick Wootton's men had creamed the absolute top odds. Officially the plunge was from 15–1 into 7–1, but *The Sydney Morning Herald* reported that some 20–1 had been available as well.

By this stage, of course, Cashy Martin's latest collection of tarp money was also safely invested. That had gone on very early, unnoticed. If only they'd been a little patient, the teenagers pondered afterwards, they might have done even better.

The Sunday News (28 April 1929): Starting from near the outside of the field, Phar Lap registered rather a good performance to win the

Rosehill Maiden Juvenile Handicap by half a length from Voleuse, with Pure Tea third. Pure Tea was a firm favourite. From No. 3 at the barrier, Pure Tea commenced well and soon drove clear of the field. Turning into the straight, Pure Tea had a lead of something like three lengths. She appeared to be going well up to the distance, but there Phar Lap challenged and while the latter was finishing solidly, Pure Tea commenced to tire. Over the last 50 yards, Pure Tea stopped to nothing and Phar Lap won by half a length from Voleuse, which finished fast from the rear of the field ...

Phar Lap is owned by the trainer, H.R. Telford, who also trains Eillom, the runner-up in the Granville Stakes. In recent years, Telford has not had anything of the class of his former charges, Ard-na-ree and Solfanello, but it is just possible that Phar Lap may be a Derby possibility ...

Most racecourses in those days, as far as punters were concerned, were divided into four areas. The racehorse owners mixed with the members and their friends in the Members' enclosure. Next in the pecking order was the 'Paddock', where well-to-do citizens mingled with some big punters as they took on the leaders of the betting ring. Down between the one- and two-furlong poles was the 'Leger' reserve, while inside the track was the 'Flat'. These areas, especially the Flat, were the domain of the working class, less courageous bookies, and children with nothing but pocket money to lose. The cost of admission, relative to the Paddock, was negligible; in fact back in the good old days you could get in for nothin' to the Flat on some courses, and racing men in Melbourne still remembered the hullabaloo from unions, the churches and the press when the VRC charged patrons a shilling to get onto the Flat for Cup Day in 1913.

Rosehill was one course without a Flat. This meant that the battling punters had no choice but to congregate together in the Leger, where weight of numbers led to many an angry scene if things didn't work out the way they were supposed to. When the favourites were losing and the weather, as it was this day, was cold and windy, the Rosehill Leger could be an unhappy place. After Phar Lap's triumph, the boys in the Leger, some of them experienced demonstrators from the Randwick Flat, were not happy. Having followed the Pure Tea money, many chastened punters now believed that Maurice McCarten, the filly's jockey, had ridden an ill-judged race and they told him so. In the mounting yard, Billy Cook, rider of Voleuse, was bemoaning a slow start, which, he told Payten and Stephen, cost him the race. Phar Lap's jockey, Jack Baker, meanwhile, reportedly remarked to Harry Telford of the race winner, 'He might be all right, as he goes well, but somehow I don't think he'll stay.'

What if Billy Cook was right, that Voleuse was a certainty beaten? Afterwards, Bayly Payten told Colin Stephen flatly, 'That's the last time that horse will ever beat Voleuse.' Or what if the angry punters were not just shouting through their pockets, and McCarten could indeed have ridden a better race on the favourite? Harry Telford, remember, was betting with money he did not have.

Tommy Woodcock: They set him for a race at Rosehill. Mr Telford got a man to back him for him, and, of course, Phar Lap did a really good thing for Mr Telford—he won, and Mr Telford won a terrible lot of money. He was a very honourable fellow, Mr Telford, and he went 'round to everybody that he owed a pound to, and he paid everybody. And after that he had very, very little left.

A tale of two Bobbies

Not long after Phar Lap returned from his 1929 winter spell, Harry Telford followed up his earlier conversation with Jim Pike, asking the great jockey if he'd ride the gelding in a bit of work to test him out for the spring. This was not a rousing gallop, just a 'nice strong effort' as Pike later called it. Hardly had the horse been pulled up and Telford wanted to know what the great rider thought. 'Harry,' Pike drawled, 'when this horse stretches out it might have the most perfect action I have ever felt. But whether that means it'll go fast, I'm not sure.'

'Will you ride him for me in the Derby?' Telford asked.

'I'll keep him in mind.'

Jim Pike hoped the horse was as good as Telford reckoned. He loved riding for the battlers, more so than for the rich men and the committee members from the racing clubs. 'I knew what want was myself,' Pike once said. And he knew Harry Telford was fair dinkum when he said he regretted that Solfanello affair.

TELFORD'S HIGH OPINION of Phar Lap surfaced again in his choice of race for Phar Lap's return as a three-year-old. The gelding, now taller and stronger but still far from regal, was entered against the older horses in the Denham Court Handicap at Warwick Farm on the first Saturday of August 1929, in which the favourite was a New Zealand-based galloper named Aussie, backed confidently on the basis of a recent victory over the weight-for-age star Limerick. The race was won, though, by Killarney, one of the best milers in training, while Phar Lap ran home encouragingly from the back of the field. No record exists of exactly where Telford's horse finished, but it could well be Phar Lap's head and soon-to-be distinctive bandaged front legs, in about tenth place, just sneaking into a photo of the finish which appeared in *The Sydney Mail*.

The run must have impressed *The Arrow*'s racing correspondent, 'Vedette', who tipped Phar Lap to his readers when the gelding returned to Rosehill a fortnight later for a seven-furlong three-year-old handicap. There was support in the bookies' ring, too, as Jim Hackett accepted a wager of £1000 to £120, and later, Joe Matthews twice held bets of £500 to £100. But this was a big betting race, with money coming for the eventual dead-heaters, King Crow and Firbolg, and also the unplaced Woodgera, who Bill Tindall had taken a huge liking to. Phar Lap, having got back early, ran right around the field to be with the leaders at the corner. According to Vedette's post-race report, Phar Lap looked the winner at the two furlongs, but the effort told and he shifted out in the straight, making a stewards' report for the first time in his life as he battled gamely for fourth, two lengths from the winners.

Although the betting money had been left in the ring, Harry Telford was excited by the run, and believed there was promise that a victory was just around the corner. On 24 August, Phar Lap stepped out in a three- and four-year-old handicap at Rosehill, and his supporters approached the race with much confidence.

C.J. Graves: My first deep impression of Phar Lap wasn't a very favourable one. Close friends of Telford gave the whisper that he was fancied for the three and four-year-old handicap, seven furlongs, at a Rosehill August meeting of 1929, and my modest pound went on at 12–1. He moved up to the lead and was one of the first three entering the straight, but as quickly faded out and missed a place, and Ticino won. It indeed was a very disappointing display from a prospective Derby candidate who was believed to be a champion in the making. But he went down in good company. Nightmarch was among the unplaced runners. Still, Nightmarch was unready and unbacked. Phar Lap was considered fit.

Nightmarch was seventh, Phar Lap eighth. Perhaps, though, the run was better than it appeared at the time, for history would show that this was a classy field. Ticino went on to run second in an Epsom Handicap. Gay Ballerina, which ran fourth in the race, later won an AJC Oaks. Cathmar, which ran fifth, would win an Epsom Handicap. And Nightmarch, the tough, classy New Zealand Derby winner of 1928, would become, with Phar Lap, the star of the 1929 spring and one of the major players in Phar Lap's extraordinary story.

TELFORD NOW TOOK what appeared on paper to be an astonishing decision to pit Phar Lap against the best horses in training in the weight-for-age Warwick Stakes. Rarely has a horse appeared more out of place—a winner of one mediocre-at-best two-year-old handicap up against Limerick and Mollison, plus Jim Pike's mount, the grand stayer Winalot, the Sydney Cup winner Crucis, the Champagne Stakes winner Parkwood, and Aussie, despite some disappointing runs in Australia, still among the favourites for the

Epsom. Telford said he was testing Phar Lap as a possible AJC Derby aspirant. What he was really doing was letting the proverbial cat out of the bag.

Truth: The surprise of the race, apart from Mollison being beaten, was the sensational finishing run of the Derby candidate, Phar Lap. He came from the rear to finish fourth, a head behind Winalot, and after the performance has come from a cricket score odds to be a fairly short one for the blue riband classic.

Jim Pike: Telford told me to keep my eye on the colt to see how he went. I saw him last behind me, early, but when I got to the post third to Limerick and Mollison, something was streaking along after me, and turning I saw it to be Phar Lap. He was only just beginning to gallop. I knew then he was going to be a champion.

Phar Lap was ridden in the Warwick Stakes, as he had been when disappointing behind Ticino at Rosehill, by Jack Brown, who won the ride after Harry Telford arrived at Randwick one morning with his two horses, Eillom and Phar Lap, but couldn't find a senior jockey to work them. After his wayward run behind King Crow and Firbolg, Telford had decided Phar Lap would go better for a stronger, more experienced jockey. 'I helped him out,' Brown told The Sun's Bill Casey in 1975. 'You couldn't see a battler stuck, could you?' Brown had won the 1925 AJC Metropolitan on Bard of Avon, and was a respected, if unfashionable, lightweight, and was in the Phar Lap saddle again for the Chelmsford Stakes, two weeks after the Warwick Stakes. But his ride was roundly criticised.

Bill Cook: It was in the 1929 Chelmsford Stakes that I had one of my greatest thrills beating Phar Lap. I had the box seat all the way on Mollison and I shot him away to a couple of lengths lead turning for home. I went past Phar Lap, who was a rangy looking three-year-old and was pocketed on the rails. I thought I was home and dried, when I heard the crowd shouting. To my amazement, I saw Phar Lap looming up beside me. I got working with hands and heels and managed to land Mollison the winner by the narrowest of margins. I realised then and there that Phar Lap was something out of the box.

Mollison had been easy in the betting ring (evens out to 2–1) and lucky on the track, as Phar Lap was caught behind tiring horses in the straight before his lightning dash at the end. This performance shot Phar Lap to the top of markets for the upcoming Rosehill Guineas, AJC Derby and, in some quarters, the Melbourne Cup. However, it also cost Jack Brown his shot at greatness. Brown had been booked for the Phar Lap ride in the Guineas, but when Telford saw what happened at Randwick, he changed his mind and turned to Jim Munro instead, for what would be the great Munro's only ride on the horse. To honour the commitment to Brown, Telford paid him £45, the equivalent of the winning jockey's fee. And that was the end of Jack Brown's association with the horse.

Truth (after the Rosehill Guineas): After being hemmed in, checked on several occasions and in an 'impossible' position at the top of the straight, Phar Lap donkey-licked the opposition over the final furlong, and won at his ease by a couple of lengths from Lorason and Holdfast ...

The crowd didn't forget to give a really great performance a really good hand, and amid a thunderclap of palm-smacking, Jim Munro brought his mount back to the enclosure.

And what a great price they got about Phar Lap yesterday ...

The *Truth* correspondent may have been talking with the precious benefit of hindsight when he lauded the bookies for their generosity. The Rosehill Guineas was, after all, only Phar Lap's second win, and it was the first time he had ever started favourite in a race. But never again would bookmakers be as generous as were those who put up 4–1 when betting on the Guineas opened. By the jump, Phar Lap was in to 2–1, which remained as good a price as you could get about the gelding on a raceday until the 1931 Melbourne Cup.

> **'Snowden' (in The Australasian):** Phar Lap is a great raking gelding. Plain maybe, compared with the colts, but withal he carries such a distinctive air of class about him for a gelding that one must indeed be hypercritical to fault him. He fills the eye for what he is, a big reachy stayer with not an ounce of lumber about him. He is a great-actioned fellow, and lopes along in effortless fashion.

The lease arrangements between David Davis and Harry Telford were that Telford would get two-thirds of the prize money and Davis one-third, Telford meeting all costs. The Guineas was worth £913 to the winner, the first big cheque of the gelding's career. However, in the betting ring Davis, with the help of some new-found big punting mates, had won much more than his share and he'd also taken some money from a couple of big off-course SP bookmakers he'd been introduced to. Now, convinced of the horse's ability and without consulting Telford, he plunged on Phar Lap in the Melbourne Cup. Telford, arguing that a hard run in the Cup might permanently damage the still-growing three-year-old, promptly told a reporter that, whatever he did in the AJC and VRC Derbies, Phar Lap would not be running in the Melbourne Cup. The press responded by challenging Telford to actually scratch the horse, rather than just talk about it. Punters wanting to wager on the Caulfield Cup–Melbourne

Cup double needed to know what the new favourite would be doing. Without this information, Cups betting was paralysed. Telford, perhaps now regretting his initial announcement, refused to make a move.

This controversy over Cups betting was just one stir to hit the racing headlines in the week before the AJC Derby. A second involved Telford's rather bizarre decision to take the Derby favourite 30 kilometres across town to Rosehill for a gallop, away from the prying eyes of the media. No-one could understand why a trainer would make a move so potentially unsettling for his horse. It seemed the pressure of finally having a top galloper might be getting to him. A third controversy concerned what had been an ongoing argument about whether geldings should be allowed to compete in these 'blue riband' classics of the Australian turf. Many in racing's highest offices, most notably the VRC chairman, Mr L.K.S. Mackinnon, contended that races such as the Derbies and Sires Produce Stakes should be kept for entires, as a means of boosting the country's breeding industry with well-credentialled locally bred sires. This debate came to a head in the spring of 1929, perhaps coincidentally, with a gelding, Phar Lap, at the head of Derby betting, ahead of Mackinnon's beautifully bred Carradale and the New Zealand wonder-colt Honour, which had won the AJC Sires Produce Stakes in the previous autumn after being purchased for a record 2300 guineas at Trentham on the same day Phar Lap was sold.

Mackinnon's prominence in the Phar Lap story was accentuated by the 1983 movie *Phar Lap*, which set him as a 'Colonel Blimp' style autocrat who would stop at next to nothing to prevent Telford's battling gelding from winning races. This picture, however, is unfair, although there is no doubt that he was a gentleman carved from the nineteenth century and he *did* dislike Harry Telford and Phar Lap. His racing colours were outrageously pretentious—white, with orange braces, orange collar, two orange armbands edged with black, and orange cap complete with silver tassle—and critics sometimes suggested that he cared little for the small punters out in the Leger and on the Flat, while worrying overly about who could get into the members' carpark. But he fought hard for Victorian racing's sake in many battles with the government, was a key figure in the introduction of a totalisator onto Melbourne racetracks and also governed the VRC bravely and shrewdly during the Depression of the early 1930s. When he died in 1935 he was given one of Melbourne's biggest funerals.

ON 5 OCTOBER 1929, Mr Mackinnon and his trainer, James Scobie, were very, very confident about Carradale's chances in the AJC Derby—a lot more sure than many of Mackinnon's business associates were about the state of the global economy, or the future of Stanley Bruce's ultra-conservative federal government, which faced an election in seven days time. Within weeks the New York Stock Exchange would crash, precipitating the Great Depression, while Bruce would lose his flash Melbourne seat as his government was decimated at the polls. These were dramatic, increasingly fragile times. At Randwick, Scobie advised an associate of the stable that something would need to run a race record to beat him, and to bet accordingly. However, after Phar Lap ran the mile and a half in 2:31.25, then the second fastest Derby win in Australian history (after Manfred's VRC Derby in 1925), to beat the glamour Victorian by three and a half lengths, Scobie confessed to reporters that 'he [Phar Lap] had made a hack of Carradale'.

A.B. Gray: My best bet on the chestnut was for the AJC Derby. Just prior to that race, he did his gallops at 10 a.m. Before coming into his own, he ran the tan circle, 7 furlongs, 95 yards, in 1:34^{1}/$_{2}$. Those who know the course will tell you what phenomenal time that is. A circle gallop means two uphill runs. He also did half a mile on the extreme outside of the course proper in 49. That was at daylight on Derby day.

Mr Gray might have been confident, but the Telfords were not. Harry's brother Hugh had come over especially for the race, but when a friend suggested that he must be confident, his reply was, 'Harry is so unlucky I can't see him ever winning good races.' Harry, for his part, thought Carradale might win. 'I'm afraid of Jim Scobie,' he confided to his brother, 'but Phar Lap is so brilliant I'm sure of winning the Craven Plate.' In the Derby, Jim Pike fought hard with Phar Lap early on, but they were helped by a filly called Queen Nassau, ridden by Rae 'Togo' Johnstone, which raced away eight lengths clear as the field headed for the back of the course. This suited the hard-fit Phar Lap more than Carradale or Honour, who had both been set for first-up victories. Johnstone was subsequently suspended for two months, for disobeying riding instructions. Pike kept a firm grip until the tearaway gave up at the three furlongs, and within a hundred yards, Phar Lap was six lengths clear and the race was won. 'Now,' wrote the Truth of Harry Telford, 'the battler's address of the future will be Easy Street.'

Peter Lawson (later trainer of 1956 Melbourne Cup winner, Evening Peal): Telford had an awful inferiority complex. Phar Lap was just coming up. The AJC Derby was really his first big race. You know what horses are like; you think you've got Tulloch in the back yard and as soon as he meets the good ones he's Michael the milkman's horse. So Harry wanted to watch the Derby from the Leger. He told me it would break the silvertails' hearts to see a battler win the Derby and he didn't want to be around to see them gloat if his horse was beaten. Phar Lap won, of course, but Harry Telford didn't go into the paddock even

then. All those photos of Phar Lap with his 'trainer' were of Hugh
Telford, Harry's brother, who had arrived from New Zealand.

As chairman of the AJC, it was Colin Stephen's job to conduct the
Derby presentation. After placing the blue riband around the neck of
the new race-record holder and warmly congratulating Hugh
Telford, he sought out his own trainer, Bayly Payten, who was
standing quietly, admiring the big chestnut. It was Payten, a little less
than six months before, after that two-year-old handicap at Rosehill,
who had told Mr Stephen that his horse, Voleuse, was better than
Phar Lap. The AJC chairman had not forgotten that remark.

'I say, Bayly,' he said seriously, 'it looks as if we have a champion
in our stable.'

AT THE SAME MEETING where Phar Lap won the AJC Derby, Eric
Connolly pulled off one of the most famous betting plunges in
Australian racing history. In the lead-up to the AJC carnival, most
observers had thought that Nightmarch was being set for the 13-
furlong Metropolitan Handicap, to be held on the Monday of the carnival, especially after Rufe Naylor had organised a big plunge with
pre-post and doubles bookmakers. Naylor thought he had reached
an understanding with Mr Louisson, the owner of Nightmarch, that
the horse would only run in the Metropolitan, and had bet accordingly. However, even as the press was reporting Naylor's activities,
Connolly was taking the top odds about Nightmarch in the Epsom
Handicap, run over a mile on the Saturday, straight after the Derby.
His bets having been placed, Connolly then offered Louisson
£10,000 for his horse, which was accepted. However, Louisson
quickly had a change of heart, and Connolly was happy to rescind the
offer, provided he could manage the horse's spring campaign. This

agreed, Connolly then gave his new partner a share of the top Epsom odds. Thus, Nightmarch was running in the mile, and his price tumbled in from 20–1 to 3–1 favourite. He duly saluted, easily by two lengths, leaving Naylor with a huge wad of worthless Epsom–Metropolitan doubles tickets.

After being 'gently' persuaded by the AJC stewards, Louisson decided to go against Connolly's advice and run Nightmarch in the Metropolitan. But Nightmarch was run down in the last furlong by Loquacious, after what many considered to be an over-confident ride by Roy Reed. Racecourse rumours suggested that Connolly had enjoyed another big win, and that Nightmarch was never supposed to run that well. It was all Reed could do to stop him getting any closer than he did.

Meanwhile, at Harry Telford's stables at Kensington, preparations were being made for Phar Lap's trip south for the Victoria Derby and then, all things going well, the Melbourne Cup. Telford retained his grave doubts about running the three-year-old in the tough two-mile classic, but his reservations were tempered by visions of the £10,000 bounty that went to the winner. Cashy Martin had no such doubts. Bobby'd murder 'em in whatever he ran in. Cashy hoped against hope that Mr Telford would send him south with the horse, to ride him in work, groom him, muck out the stables, keep guard, anything ...

Nightmarch headed to Melbourne straight after the Metropolitan. Not long after, having trounced Mollison on a bog track in the Craven Plate, Phar Lap followed, accompanied not by Cashy Martin but by Tommy Woodcock. To this point in Phar Lap's racing career, while Woodcock had helped the once-struggling Telford as much as he could, the gelding's most regular attendant on racedays had been Tommy Sumner. In fact, Sumner fulfilled the strapper's role on AJC Derby day, and received a £10 'sling' from Telford after the race.

However, the canny trainer had noticed the affinity between Woodcock and his horse, and immediately after the Derby, with his two-thirds share of the winner's cheque in his pocket, Telford invited the 23-year-old to be his full-time stable foreman, and take his Melbourne Cup favourite south. Woodcock couldn't say yes quickly enough.

As a racing man, Woodcock was the complete antithesis of Pike and Telford. Whereas jockey and trainer captured in their aged appearances the tough times of the Depression—Pike especially so with his gaunt look from years of wasting to ride at weights his body didn't like—Tommy looked positively angelic. He was a thin little man, just too big to be the jockey he'd hoped to be as a boy, who always looked even smaller on race days, hidden as he was beside his giant horse and beneath his colossal felt hat. Shy, and confident only with horses, he wanted to be stylish but had no idea exactly how to pull it off. He didn't drink, was always polite and softly spoken, and knew his place. Fifty years later, when he re-entered the media spotlight by training a horse called Reckless to nearly win a Melbourne Cup, women half his age wanted to mother him. But Tommy didn't need mothering; it just looked that way to observers who from a distance never saw him, mud on rolled-up sleeves, working with the angriest horses in the yards.

Jim Pike: I remember riding Phar Lap round the tracks at Randwick one morning when I realised there was something wrong with him. He had taken his attention off his work. I couldn't see any reason; there was nobody around. But suddenly, when we got around a turn, we spotted Tommy Woodcock, his attendant, in the distance. Phar Lap had sensed his presence. Nothing would do but we must pull up and go over to him, and Tommy had to quickly pick a piece of grass and give it to him.

Whether, after arriving in Melbourne in mid-October 1929, Woodcock was still excited about his new job is problematical, for no sooner had Phar Lap headed to his temporary home at Caulfield trainer Joe Cripps' stables than the horse was running a fever. Telford dashed south earlier than he'd intended. But although Phar Lap missed a few days' work, by the last week of October, the seven days leading up to the Victoria Derby at Flemington, most reporters were convinced the report of the Cup favourite's cold was just another furphy, aimed at building publicity and confusing the press, the bookmakers and the betting public.

'Panacre' (in The Arrow): The rumour he was possessed of a cold and would be unlikely to contest the Victorian classic had a regular Melburnian touch, for that city is renowned for its scares on the eve of the big spring fixtures. Apparently it is an heirloom from the old country, where international crooks are credited with designs on the favourite very often—possibly in the interests of melodrama.

Subsequent tales from the Telford camp would reveal, however, that the reports were fair dinkum. The sick horse had missed some work. Noted veterinary surgeon Dr W.J. Stewart McKay, who would devote a great deal of his time and writing over the following three years to the champion, reckoned the 'influenza', as he called it, and the work they pumped into the three-year-old once he was healthy again, hurt the horse more than the stable realised.

On the Saturday before the Derby, the same day Nightmarch was winning the Cox Plate at Moonee Valley, Phar Lap was introduced to the man who would ride him in the Cup, the veteran Bobby Lewis. It had only been in the previous week that Telford had finally confirmed Phar Lap's involvement in the Cup. Originally, Phar Lap was weighted in the Cup to carry only 6.12. However, if he won either the

AJC or VRC Derbies (or both) his Cup weight, according to the conditions of the race, would be 7.6, weight-for-age for a three-year-old colt. There was no way Jim Pike could make that sort of weight. Originally, Telford leaned towards using a Sydney lightweight such as Ted Bartle or Billy Cook, and even invited Cook to ride the gelding in trackwork at Caulfield. A mix-up in times, however, meant Cook left the course before Woodcock and Phar Lap arrived—and left the jockey regretting his impatience for the rest of his life. Eventually, Telford opted for the experience and home-town knowledge of the local man, and on that Saturday, with stablemate Eillom to keep them company over the final three furlongs, Phar Lap and Lewis galloped sedately over a mile and three-quarters. 'Judging by the manner in which he went for Lewis,' wired 'Clifden' to The Referee, 'rider and horse were suited from the start.'

PHAR LAP AND NIGHTMARCH, in that order, dominated Cup betting, with the Caulfield Cup winner, High Syce, and the Moonee Valley Cup winner, Prince Viol, the only other contenders. 'The way they are backing Nightmarch and High Syce suggests that all is not well with the favourite,' one leading operator told the Pictorial. But the paper also quoted a source from the Phar Lap camp saying, 'Telford advised me not to hedge my bets.' By the Tuesday before the Cup, a week before the jump, only sixteen of the original 325 entries remained in the field. This, The Sydney Morning Herald's correspondent suggested, reflecting the increasingly trying times, was because 'many owners have realised the futility of paying the £75 sweepstake for the purpose of having their colours carried in the historic race'. The 1929 field would be the second smallest in Cup history.

First to the Victoria Derby, which was watched by a crowd of more than 60,000—down on previous years, it was noted—enjoying a magnificent Melbourne day. Phar Lap arrived at Flemington late and accompanied by a special police guard after rumours reached Telford that someone might try to get at the gelding. Despite such talk and the speculation concerning his health, Phar Lap opened at 4–1 on and very quickly firmed in to 5–1 on, before starting at 9–2 on. And he won as he liked, smashing the great Manfred's race record in the process. Even so, after the race Pike told reporters he felt the horse was not quite as good or as tractable as he had been in Sydney.

Jim Pike: The colt is not used to a walk-up start and that was why
he was slow away. The field got a bit of a break on him at the barrier.
I eased him up behind them until he started to fight for his head.
At the mile and a quarter I let him go a bit faster. Then he went up on
the outside of two horses. From that point the race was not in doubt.

Given he missed the start, Phar Lap's time was phenomenal. The last half mile was run in 47$^{1}/_{2}$ seconds—three-quarters of a second quicker than the older Amounis' last half mile in the one-mile Cantala Stakes on the same program—as Telford's rising star ran along in the straight at his own pace to win by two lengths from Carradale, thus again thwarting L.K.S. Mackinnon's long-held ambition to win a Derby. In the Melbourne Stakes, Nightmarch appeared a tad unlucky in finishing only third behind High Syce and Mollison, while Prince Viol was injured when running third behind Shadow King in the Hotham Handicap. By the time the bookies packed up their bags, Phar Lap was rock-solid as Cup favourite, with High Syce a clear second pick. But on the Monday, there was considerable backing for two others—Nightmarch and Carradale.

Carradale had been backed significantly in Cups doubles, and it seemed most of his support came from doubles bookmakers trying to balance their accounts. The Nightmarch plunge was led, inevitably, by Eric Connolly. It was rumoured that he had tried to convince Mr Louisson that Jim Pike, and not Roy Reed, should ride the horse, but Louisson stuck solid with his jockey. Afterwards, it was suggested that Connolly's heavy support for Nightmarch was based on a conversation he had had with Pike, in which the Derby-winning rider had explained that Phar Lap had pulled very hard throughout most of the first half of the classic. Pike was just about the strongest jockey on the planet; Connolly's theory was that if Pike had trouble holding the three-year-old then the veteran Lewis would definitely struggle. But other reports, while estimating that Connolly might win as much as £50,000, also intimated that he'd supported Phar Lap strongly from the time the three-year-old ran second in the Chelmsford Stakes.

Racing sages pointed to the Cup experiences of Manfred (1925) and Strephon (1928), who had spreadeagled their Derby opponents but finished only second in the Cup on the following Tuesday. In fact, of the nineteen dual Derby winners to run in the Melbourne Cup to that point, only four—Grand Flaneur (1880), Poseidon (1906), Prince Foote (1909) and Trivalve (1927)—had completed the treble. Lewis, however, would have none of such pessimism. 'I think I will have the goods under me this time, all right,' he told reporters. The betting moves in the half hour before the race were all for the favourite, who firmed from 6–4 to evens, the shortest price ever bet to that time in the Melbourne Cup. At the same time, Carradale kept firming, from 12–1 into 7s. But Nightmarch was easy, 4s out to 6s, suggesting that whatever the size of Connolly's investment on the horse, it hadn't been enough to put a major dent in the ring.

As the horses headed for the jump, it was clear that Lewis was finding Phar Lap to be a real handful ...

The Sydney Morning Herald: It was an overcoated and warmly-wrapped crowd, equipped apparently to a man with umbrellas which, from the heights surrounding the Flemington racecourse, saw Nightmarch and Paquito rob Phar Lap of victory in the last stages of the Melbourne Cup race this afternoon. Swept by a bitterly cold wind, occasionally under drizzling rain, and inhabited by a crowd which took its pleasure most seriously, Flemington was not a very attractive spot. In the circumstances it was surprising that the crowd numbered probably 100,000, not including those less well-endowed thousands who were content, perforce, to choose Scotsman's Hill and other vantage points outside the racecourse from which to view the race.

Bobby Lewis: I didn't want the lead at the start, but I was on the rails and the colt sprung out well. Then I tried to get in behind Taisho, but it ran off and there I was left in front. Nothing would pass me. The worst of it was that Phar Lap kept his head up and back. I couldn't hold him in like that. If he had had his head down I could have: but as it was I was getting a very jerky ride. He was bounding along like a kangaroo and fighting all the time. I tried to get his head down, but I could not, whatever I did. All this was taking a terrible lot off the horse and so I finally let him stride along and get a break on the field. It was the best thing I could think of to do in the circumstances and then, of course, you know he did not have enough left in the straight.

Tommy Woodcock: Bobby Lewis was a top lightweight jockey. You couldn't take that away from him, but the horse didn't like him and he pulled that hard with him that poor horse had cuts in his mouth and he slobbered and he could hardly eat anything for three or four days after.

Back in Sydney, Cashy Martin was listening to the live broadcast on Radio 2FC, occasionally switching to 2BL to see if the reception was any better there. Before the start he was supremely confident, but as soon as he heard, after two furlongs, the race commentator say, 'Phar Lap's fighting for his head,' he began to worry. Straight afterwards, he couldn't believe it. 'Must 'ave been a fix, the boss shouldn't 'ave put a Victorian on 'im!' he cried. Many others immediately thought the same thing, hardly believing that the phenomenon who'd won the Derby so easily could this time have compounded in the straight. Some spoke suspiciously about the money that had come for Carradale and the fact that Scobie and Lewis had been close associates for years. Others looked at Connolly, his Nightmarch betting tickets and the fact he was a friend of Lewis. But Cashy Martin's good friend Jim Marsh and Stewart McKay had different views.

Jim Marsh: I did see that Melbourne Cup. Phar Lap did the same that day as what he'd later do with Billy Elliott in the two-and-a-quarter mile race at Randwick when he broke every record. Where Lewis made the mistake was that he hung on to him and hung on to him until about seven furlongs from home. When he bolted on little Elliott, he just let him go and he kept on going for two-and-a-quarter miles. That's what he would've done in the Cup, if Lewis had let him go. But you can't blame Lewis for it, he was trying to do the best he could. There's no way a jockey could let a horse go at its top all the way in the Melbourne Cup.

W.J. Stewart McKay: In the Cup Phar Lap was very excited, perhaps he had taken 'tonics' to help him and had then been over excited, for in the race he ran like a horse that was 'possessed', and fought like a demon. And so his brain batteries and his heart gave out and he pulled up a very tired horse, and poor old Bobby Lewis was reviled most unjustly. Let us hope that the race has done Phar Lap no harm. Time alone will tell us.

In an interview the following year, Telford admitted that, with hindsight, his instructions to Lewis were wrong, and that the jockey, in restraining Phar Lap, was simply doing as he was told. 'Supposing they walk?' Lewis had asked Telford before the race. 'You walk, too,' was the trainer's terse reply. 'If you are near the leaders half a mile from home, nothing can take the race away.'

After the race, though, all Telford said to reporters, once they had finished talking with the winning connections, was, 'It is bad luck that the slowly run race beat my horse.'

Perhaps Lewis' biggest mistake—but how was he to know?—was that he bustled the horse from the jump, to avoid a potential scrimmage. Phar Lap had drawn the rails. In his previous runs Jim Pike, and Jim Munro in the Rosehill Guineas, had let the horse get balanced before asking for anything. Here, Lewis, having fired him up to get forward, then fought to slow him down and didn't let him go until the end of the back straight, when he quickly opened up a three-length lead. Shadow King loomed up as the field commenced the sweeping turn into the straight, and then Carradale made a dash at the lead. Phar Lap seemed spent, exhausted by his antics. But just as the crowd yelled out that the favourite was beaten, Mr Mackinnon's hope ran off the track towards the outside rail (searching, Scobie suggested later, for where he headed off the course every morning after trackwork) leaving Phar Lap still in front with two furlongs to go. But then Roy Reed on Nightmarch said go and the Kiwi champion exploded away. He dashed over the last half-mile in 47$\frac{1}{2}$ seconds—the fastest four furlongs in Cup history—revealing both his great staying prowess and the farcical early pace. Meanwhile, Maurice McCarten on Paquito was cutting Phar Lap out of second prize.

The general consensus afterwards was that Phar Lap was probably not quite as good as his Derby wins had led everyone to believe. Vedette in The Referee wrote, 'Given a spell, Phar Lap is likely to develop into a really great horse by the autumn. He may not have another opportunity of winning the Melbourne Cup and other big handicaps, but is sure to keep the world from the door in set weight events.' Snowden in *The Australasian* was even less impressed, arguing, 'Phar Lap is a good average Derby winner, but no regrets should be expressed that he is a gelding.'

AFTER A STRONG media debate over Lewis' ride finally died down, there was still one more controversy to overcome before Phar Lap could head off for a well-earned spell. Come Friday morning, both Nightmarch and Phar Lap were still in the C.B. Fisher Plate, a mile-and-a-half race run on the final Saturday of the carnival. During the day, Nightmarch was withdrawn. On the Saturday, Telford and Phar Lap went to the course, seemingly ready to race, but around one o'clock the dual-Derby winner was sensationally withdrawn, allegedly following a conversation between Telford, Eric Connolly and David Davis. Connolly was soon seen rushing for the betting ring, where he plunged successfully on Amounis to beat the only other starters, High Syce and Carradale.

Davis had been very impressed with the way Connolly had manip-ulated the bookmakers throughout the spring, and the way he built on successes, one after the other. Connolly was impressed with the fact that Davis owned the best young racehorse in the country. The two, it seemed, were now firm friends.

Meanwhile, Harry Telford had learned about a training facility that was being offered for leasing for five years by the Melbourne and Metropolitan Board of Works, the water supply and sewerage works authority. On the Friday before the Fisher Plate he'd headed out to inspect the 143-acre farm, called 'Braeside', which was located on the lower Dandenong Road at Mordialloc, south-east of the city and about three miles from the Mentone and Epsom racecourses. Previously, this had been the private domain of Dr A.E. Syme, a thoroughbred breeder and enthusiast who raced horses under the pseudonym 'S.A. Rawdon', but he had sold it to the Melbourne and Metropolitan Board of Works. Now it became the establishment of one Mr H.R. Telford. Reaping the rewards of the great Phar Lap harvest, Telford would build Braeside into an impressive ultra-private training centre, home for the thirty or more young horses that would come under his care in the following eighteen months. The tiny old stables in Bowral Street were left behind, Sydney and the creditors who'd made life so hard for him far away and forgotten.

CASHY MARTIN WAS DEVASTATED when he learnt of Mr Telford's plans. Then exhilarated when the boss asked him to follow him to Melbourne. Then shattered again when his mother blocked the move. 'But, Mum, it's the chance of a lifetime,' he cried.

'I'm sorry, Mr Telford, but at least for the moment, I think Cash should stay here with me.' Mrs Martin ignored the teenager's pleas, looking instead at Telford, who sipped carefully at his tea, new felt hat sitting in front of him on the kitchen table.

'If that's your wish,' Telford replied. 'Perhaps, though, if it's okay with you, Cash could come to Melbourne during January, and ride the big horse in work. It'd be a good experience for the lad. Good for the horse, too.'

Mrs Martin said she'd think about it. Meanwhile, Cashy's indentures were transferred to another Randwick trainer, J.H. 'Jack' Munro, elder brother of the jockeys Jim and Darby. And it was for Jack Munro, just days later on 1 December 1929, that H.C. Martin, claimin' seven, rode his first winner, a two-year-old called La Gloria.

When betting opened, La Gloria was 4–1, but she eased dramatically while the favourite, Going On, ridden by Jim Munro, was never better than 2s.

> **Truth (1 December 1929):** There were dozen of punters who rushed in with their heads down to back La Gloria, never bothering to look at the semaphore to see who was aboard the filly. There were also hundreds of wary ones who took the precaution of scanning the board to see who had the mounts. They immediately allowed La Gloria to run against them ...
>
> Both La Gloria and Going On were drawn near the rails, but young Martin showed more enterprise at the start by bouncing La Gloria to the front. But it was not long before Jimmy Munro had his mount pinned to the heels of La Gloria, and just as the field swung into the straight La Gloria went wide and allowed Going On to shoot through up the fence and secure the lead. Up went the cry, 'The favourite's home!'—it certainly looked like it, for Going On had a length's break on brother Jackie's charge, and La Gloria was by this time in the centre of the track, having lost lengths. But with 100 yards to go, Going On, ridden frantically by Jimmy Munro, had shot everything in his locker, and La Gloria, with young Martin anxiously looking at the favourite, came along again with a wet sail and went by Going On to win by half a length.

Mr Munro had explained to Cashy that the horse would probably hang in the straight. For a couple of years, Mr Telford had been telling Cashy to never panic, a message the little apprentice remembered in the straight, when Jim Munro snuck inside him. Given the drift in the betting, there was little applause as he came back to scale, only the rousing cheers of his Kenso mates, the satisfied smile of a proud mother, and, at the back of the mounting yard, perhaps the hint of a grin from the trainer of Phar Lap.

He could've won by a furlong

Phar Lap spelled over summer at Mr Sol Green's magnificent property, 'Underbank', which was situated at Bacchus Marsh, around 50 kilometres north-east of Melbourne. Sol Green was a Londoner who had sailed to Australia in 1885 with no money in his pockets, but plenty of spunk and ambition. Eventually, he became the owner of Comedy King, winner of the Melbourne Cup in 1910, plus a number of other crack gallopers including the weight-for-age specialist Gothic, the mare Gladsome and the brilliant colt Strephon. As well he was a flamboyant bookmaker, with a penchant for Havana cigars and Rolls Royces. His estate was extraordinary—speculation had it that Green had spent upwards of £200 an acre on it, to the point of monitoring the creeks to ensure the horses were getting the best possible drinking water. However, earlier in the year Green had sold all his thoroughbreds bar Strephon (which he'd sent to England to try to win the Ascot Gold Cup), after a stewards' inquiry unfairly, in his view, impugned his reputation. Thus there was plenty of room in the stables. He respected Telford as a horseman, like many in racing was taken by Telford's new champion, and was more than happy to be of service. Not that Phar Lap was the only champion to go there. Frank McGrath, the trainer of Amounis, had been taking advantage of Mr Green's hospitality for years. To Telford, Underbank was so far from the sandhills south of Kensington it wasn't funny. Woodcock, ever faithful to the horse, went to Underbank too and rigged a hammock next to Phar Lap's box so he could tend to his friend's every need.

Tommy Woodcock: We was up there for six weeks, and Phar Lap, you wouldn't know him. Aw, he come back a robust sort of horse. He was really good. He got stronger, much stronger with his spell up at the beautiful paddocks, and the beautiful grass, and with a real rest from everything. Aw, he put on a lot of condition and got to be a big strong horse, 'specially when I was giving him a bit of exercise 'round the hills. I think it did develop him a terrible lot for the autumn. He never looked back after that.

Cashy left for Melbourne in the first week of 1930, the same week Phar Lap returned to Joe Cripps' stables at Caulfield. Telford's ambition was to have Braeside ready by the end of the autumn. Cashy rode the gelding in all its work throughout the month, not returning to Sydney until early February, by which time the horse was preparing for a first-up battle with Amounis in the St George Stakes. With Pike unavailable, Telford again gave the ride to Bobby Lewis.

Jim Pike: When I met Harry Telford on arrival in Melbourne that year he wanted me to ride Phar Lap for the St George Stakes, WFA, at the Caulfield Autumn meeting, but I had been engaged for Amounis, so, of course, I had to stick to him. Harry didn't worry though. He told me that he didn't think Phar Lap was ready to win it, and, in fact, had little or no chance because he was a bit backward in condition and I needn't worry. [But] I was to ride Phar Lap in the Leger a fortnight after and he thought the ride might be useful.

Whatever Telford's opinion, there was money for Phar Lap, in from 2s to 7–4. But the older horse won easily, prompting Musket in *The Sydney Mail* to write that Phar Lap was 'not a champion—else he would have made Amounis stretch out to beat him'.

These two horses, one seven years old and the other three, went on to dominate the Victorian autumn. Amounis won three races after the St George Stakes—the Futurity Stakes, the Essendon Stakes and the C.M. Lloyd Stakes—while Phar Lap added the three-year-old classic, the St Leger, to his résumé and then easily won the longer WFA races, the Governor's Plate and the King's Plate. In the St Leger a race-course rumour that all was not well saw his price drift from 7–1 on to 2–1 on, with a dash of 7–4 on available at post time. Telford admitted afterwards that while Phar Lap was very healthy, with an eye to the demanding schedule the horse had in front of him he had given him an easy time since the first-up run at Caulfield. By the two-mile King's Plate, however, Phar Lap was closer to his top, and won by twenty lengths, at 10–1 on, after leading by half a furlong at the mile post.

AND SO TO SYDNEY, for the first time since the previous October. On his first look at him, Vedette in *The Referee* wrote, 'Since he was here in the spring Phar Lap has furnished into a much more impressive type of horse. Never an oil painting, he is not the pretty type, but he fills the eye with his bigness, his undoubted physical fitness and his general air of contentedness and well-being.' 'Musket', in *The Sydney Mail*, added, 'Were it not for his wonderful deeds few would take a second look at him; but now that he has become famous his rangy frame of greyhound proportions has many admirers.' The Sydney press had a field day building up the Chipping Norton Stakes, over a mile and a quarter at Warwick Farm on 12 April, in which Phar Lap would meet Amounis, Nightmarch and another outstanding Kiwi,

Chide. David Davis couldn't wait. Eric Connolly told him that Sydney's biggest female punter, Maude Vandenburg, was going to back her personal favourite, Amounis, on which she'd won a serious amount of money in the past. Davis would have a chance to get a price about his horse, and make some serious money too.

> **Musket:** Five furlongs from home, Nightmarch appeared to be catching the three-year-old, but it was only on sufferance, for the gap became wider at the three furlongs, where Amounis began to close on Nightmarch. 'Amounis will win yet!' was shouted by his admirers as the old warrior began his famous finishing run, but though he caught Nightmarch he could not threaten danger to the three-year-old, who simply outclassed the placegetters.

'That settles which horse should've won the Melbourne Cup!' yelled a voice from the Leger. Racing had a new hero, and he couldn't have come at a better time, with thousands losing their jobs and the papers filling with bleak stories of hardship and misfortune. The Scullin Labor Government, elected amid hope the previous October, was now floundering, failing to gain the support of the upper class for their reforms, which made ineffective their efforts to ease the impact of the recession. City hotels that were usually booked out were cutting their rates, as country folk stayed home to ponder their dilemmas. 'As a rule,' commented The Australasian, 'Easter is a period of gaiety and festivity in Sydney. [However] the carnival spirit this year will not be so free because at present most people are lamenting the scarcity of money.'

The irony of Harry Telford's new-found wealth could not have been lost on him. Circumstances had changed drastically for both him and the world around him. Men who only a year previously had been calling in Telford debts were now seeking a handout. A few months earlier he had watched the AJC Derby from the Leger—to avoid people he saw as snobs. Now some of those snobs were stuck in the Leger themselves. Easy wins in the AJC St Leger and the weight-for-age Cumberland Stakes followed, after which it was generally considered that Phar Lap was the equal of any of the great three-year-olds of the previous thirty years, such as Abundance, Poseidon, Mountain King, Prince Foote, Artilleryman, Manfred and Strephon. Similarly, it was now being suggested that 21-year-old Don Bradman, who three months before had broken the record for the highest score ever made in first-class cricket, was now on a par with the great Australian batsmen of the past, including Charlie Bannerman, Clem Hill, Victor Trumper and Bill Ponsford.

IF YOU TALK to anyone in Sydney who saw most of Phar Lap's races, the one performance they all truly rave about is the AJC Plate, run at Randwick over two-and-a-quarter miles on 26 April.

The headlines immediately afterwards were astonishingly exuberant: 'GREATEST HORSE EVER,' roared Truth. 'PHAR LAP MOST SENSATIONAL GALLOPER OF ALL TIME,' shouted The Referee. 'AN EXTRAORDINARY WIN' was The Australasian's verdict. 'PHAR LAP SUPERLATIVE GALLOPER,' reckoned The Sydney Mail.

What Telford's gelding had done was take hold of Billy Elliott, up from Melbourne for the ride because Jim Pike couldn't make the three-year-old's weight-for-age of 7.13, and take off. The pace was suicidal for a normal horse, but Phar Lap kept going and going, until Elliott finally managed to ease him up over the last furlong. Before the race—which involved only three horses, Phar Lap, Nightmarch and the solid stayer Donald (a fourth acceptor, Kikaides, was scratched)—some critics thought Nightmarch might be a chance. After all, he'd beaten the three-year-old easily in the Melbourne Cup and their only subsequent meeting had been over a mile and a quarter in the Chipping Norton Stakes. There was talk about, according to *Truth*, that Phar Lap 'was going to be raced right into the ground'. Consequently, he came up only 2–1 on in the ring, but the big punters were onto that in a flash, with Maude Vandenburg quickly taking £2000 to £1000 from rails operator Jack Molloy. Eric Connolly, however, was spotted supporting Nightmarch. At the jump, Phar Lap was 5–2 on.

'Chiron' (in The Australasian): Evidently the people who backed Nightmarch took the view that Phar Lap is really not a genuine stayer and that Nightmarch would be able to get the last run on him and outstay him at the finish. It did not work out that way at all, as Nightmarch could never get near enough to Phar Lap to find out whether he can stay or not.

Vedette: Phar Lap went fast from the beginning and some of his intermediate times from a mile and a half on, according to private watches, were better than world figures for those distances. The full time of 3:49.5 was a second better than the previous Australasian record and he beat Nightmarch by 10 lengths, with Donald three-quarters of a length away third. He clipped the previous Randwick record by 6$\frac{1}{2}$ seconds.

An English writer a few weeks ago mentioned that Walter Lindrum [the champion Australian billiards exponent] was the only man in any branch of sport he would be prepared to back against the world. Sydney sportsmen who saw Phar Lap's performance in the AJC Plate were convinced he is the Lindrum of the turf. It is difficult to make comparisons between Australian and overseas horses, but when a galloper arises who can make really good performers such as Nightmarch look like novices, there is no question of his class.

The first half mile was run in 49 seconds. In a two-and-a-quarter-mile race! The previous November, Nightmarch had run the last half mile of his Melbourne Cup in a record 47½ seconds. To run this sort of pace at the start of a staying test was ridiculous. Along the back, still more than a mile from home, Phar Lap was ticking over the furlongs twelve seconds at a time, as he opened up a lead of at least a furlong, perhaps longer. Vedette's stopwatch suggested he ran the first seven furlongs in better than the Randwick track record, equal to the Australasian record, for THAT distance. In a two-and-a-quarter-mile race!!

Jim Pike (interviewed after the race): Phar Lap is faster than Strephon. Much faster. Windbag could win a six-furlongs race and the Melbourne Cup. Gothic won two VRC Newmarket Handicaps and could stay a mile and a half, but I have no hesitation in saying that up to a mile and a half Phar Lap is better and could outpace either of them from anything up to that distance. I feel sure he could win a Newmarket, and win it easily. And I would not hesitate to back him, fit and at his best, to run a mile and a half in 2.27. That's how good I think he is.

Phar Lap had run the first mile and a half of the AJC Plate in 2:28.5, nearly three seconds faster than the race-record time he ran to win the AJC Derby seven months before. Two miles were passed in 3:20½, which would have won every Sydney Cup until 1971, and every Melbourne Cup until 1950, at which point Elliott was finally able to get a grip, and he slowed the champion down to a canter in the straight, while Nightmarch and Donald were ridden hard, chasing the second prize money. So slowly was Phar Lap going at the finish that he was walking, ready to enter the mounting yard, only 25 metres after passing the post.

Jim Marsh: He could've won by a furlong. Roy Reed rode Nightmarch and afterwards the stewards got him up before them on a charge of not riding his mount out. He'd got beat a furlong! The judge didn't say that was the margin, but that's what it looked like to me. What Reed did was get half a length in front of Donald, then he just looked at him and stayed there. He didn't try to run after Phar Lap, that was true, and he explained that to the stewards. 'I could have run him to about 50 lengths,' he said. All he wanted to do was beat Donald.

A. McAulay (trainer of Nightmarch): It is hard to say what would have been the result if Phar Lap had been asked to do his best: Nightmarch would hardly have been at the home turn when the crack finished.

It was, by any measure, a remarkable win, unique in Australian racing history. Although Phar Lap was still to go to Adelaide for their autumn carnival, the AJC Plate was the crowning statement on his sensational three-year-old season. His domination of the Randwick carnival was the feature of what was otherwise a somewhat depressing week, in which crowds and betting turnover were down and the AJC chairman, Colin Stephen, at a meeting of the Bloodhorse Breeders' Association, strongly hinted that prize money for the big races would have to be cut.

PHAR LAP'S ADELAIDE TRIP came about after an invitation from the South Australian Jockey Club, which suited Telford, who was aware that his lease of Phar Lap would run out the following February and thus wanted to chase as much stakes money as he could. And the idea of the trip quickly suited David Davis too, once he worked out a way to significantly benefit from the adventure. The scam was simple: Telford had entered Phar Lap in three races over the SAJC carnival—the Elder Stakes, the Adelaide Cup and the King's Cup. Unless something strange happened, he had no intention of running the horse in the Adelaide Cup for Telford feared running the three-year-old over two miles with a big weight. The SAJC handicapper, none other than the former Test cricket champion Clem Hill, gave Phar Lap 9.8, more than a stone heavier than any other final acceptor in the race, the other entries being headed by the five-year-old mare Nadean, the recent Australian Cup winner. But the other two races would be easy pickings, and with the locals covering expenses, Telford would pick up another 1000 quid. Davis knew that on-course bookmakers were banned in South Australia, with punters restricted to betting on the tote machine or with the illegal SP operators off-course. And he knew what to do—he'd seen it done in California many times before.

'I don't want to know what you're doing,' was all Telford said to him.

Phar Lap was greeted by around 100 people when he arrived at Adelaide railway station. Six days later, he lured a bigger than usual crowd to Morphettville for the Elder Stakes meeting, although *The Advertiser*'s racing correspondent bemoaned the fact that so few inter-state horses were competing—most, it seems, scared away by Phar Lap's presence—and that tote turnover was down. This, he commented, was a reflection on 'the effects of the financial depression'. The same reporter was hardly overwhelmed by the champion's looks. 'If you saw him run unplaced in a trial stakes,' he sneered, 'you'd say over hurdles is his game.'

For the main race of the day there were only two contenders—Phar Lap and the local mare Fruition. No-one thought she had a chance and early betting reflected this. In fact, because of the 12.5

per cent deduction on all investments (some to go the SAJC, the rest to the state government's tax coffers), most shied away from wagering at all, fearing that even if they backed Phar Lap and he won they might get back less than what they put on. But then, in the last minutes of betting, something very weird happened.

The Advertiser: Bystanders who were watching the totalisator noticed the addition of 200 5/- units to the total, with the result that Phar Lap was showing a dividend of £1 12/-. The start was to be made at any moment and a number of people rushed the windows. In a moment or two the dividend was reduced to £1 6/- and the totalisator closed.

Someone had put a ridiculously large wager on Fruition. When the person involved was cornered, he explained, somewhat sheepishly, that he'd assumed Phar Lap was No. 1 and bet accordingly. It was not until too late that he realised that, because this was a weight-for-age event, the older mare carried more weight than the three-year-old gelding and was consequently the topweight.

A likely story, thought the cynical Sydney newshounds, who quickly discovered that SP bookies across the country had become the victims of a 'sting', having been obliged to pay out on the odds equivalent—around 3–1 on—of the final totalisator dividend. But the damage, according to the Sydney *Sportsman*, was not too great. The paper ridiculed Davis, rather than elevating him to the status of the racing game's biggest schemers. Remembering a similar rort that had been worked on a race at the New South Wales provincial track at Kembla Grange, back during a brief spell when tote betting was compulsory, the paper commented that 'only the veriest novice at SP-ing will now accept wagers at machine odds'. The paper concluded by saying, 'Seeing that Phar Lap paid only £1 6/- for a quid the Adelaide "jokers" didn't work their scheme nearly as well as they might have.'

A much bigger storm struck on the Wednesday, Adelaide Cup day. Although Telford continued to say that Phar Lap was a very doubtful runner in the race, he did pay the £15 final acceptance fee on the Monday, which led many locals to conclude that the horse was going to be the star attraction of the big day. Or was he? At 1.10 on race afternoon, having fought his way through the long queues waiting to get in to see his champion, Telford went to the SAJC offices and took his horse out of the Cup. Once word of this development got out, angry patrons gathered to vent their dissatisfaction. Police advised the authorities to forget a plan to parade the gelding down the home straight, and when a big chestnut horse that might have been Phar Lap—but was actually a roughie called Amant—was led into the mounting yard it was roundly booed. Not all of these protesters were on the Flat, noted The Advertiser's correspondent: many were in the grandstand enclosure. Afterwards, Telford admitted he had left the decision to the last minute so that the Club, which was paying his way, would get as large a gate as possible. This didn't help matters. As the editorial writers quickly noted, while the SAJC might have appreciated the gesture, many other not-so-well-off racing folk would not have been so grateful.

On the following Saturday, Phar Lap won the King's Cup comfortably, carrying 17 lb over weight-for-age, but the victory was hardly celebrated as it might have been. While many in the stands politely applauded the horse down the straight, the people on the Flat watched in stony silence. All up, while Telford had won more than £1000 in stakes money and Davis had enjoyed his betting 'coup', the trip to Adelaide had hardly been a brilliant public relations exercise.

Telford now headed to Braeside, officially set up as his headquarters, while Phar Lap and Woodcock were given another holiday at Sol Green's Underbank. Spell over they too would go to Braeside, to be domiciled under the same expansive roof as around twenty young thoroughbreds, most of them purchased by Telford on behalf of a mysterious group of owners who operated under the nom-de-plume 'F. Smithden', at either the January Trentham or April Sydney sales. All up, Telford had spent over £12,000 of his new connections' money on these yearlings. Of the splendidly developed property he and his family now called home, Telford wryly muttered one day, 'I'll need three Phar Laps to pay for all this.' When Cashy Martin came down in July to check the joint out and ride some of the youngsters in work, he looked around at the manicured lawns and painstakingly restored stables, grinned at Mr Telford, and said, 'Geez, boss, it's a helluva long way from Bowral Street!'

BEFORE THE TUMULTUOUS 1929–30 racing season had ended, the VRC and AJC had agreed to introduce the often-mooted ban on geldings for their two-year-old and three-year-old classics. A joint statement from the two clubs began: 'The committees are of the opinion that if horse racing is to fulfil its primary objective, which is to improve the breed of horses, it is not likely to achieve that end by allowing geldings to run in such highly endowed races as the Sires Produce Stakes for two-year-olds and the Derbies and St Legers for three-year-olds ...' Many observers concluded this was simply a reaction to Phar Lap's domination, but given that the matter had been a public issue for years, and that in barring geldings Australian authorities were merely bringing local racing into line with the situation in the UK, this was unfair. From 1932–33, geldings were out, and they stayed out until 1957.

Whether it was a clever move was debatable, however, and many in racing criticised the initiative. The ambition behind the strategy was to increase the number of credentialled Australian-bred stallions—owners were more likely to send their mares to a Derby winner than to a horse that had been beaten in the race by one or more geldings. And there was always that regret that a champion gelding wasn't able to pass on his blood to future generations. But as we have seen, when Telford decided to geld Phar Lap he did so because he believed the horse would handle the rigours of racing much better if the operation was done. Had he not been gelded, he might not have seen the racetrack, or been tractable or any good once he got there. Bill Kelso, the trainer of the 1928 Melbourne Cup winner, Statesman, (who was gelded after his Cup win!) reckoned in the main that 'geldings race more honestly, are easier to train, easier to handle in the stable and easier to spell'. Another veteran leading trainer, Frank Marsden, mentor of the outstanding Derby winners Furious and Richmond Main, pointed to a number of high-class geldings, including Phar Lap, Gloaming and Amounis, and suggested that the ban could lead to fewer superstars and consequently lower the quality of racing.

'The principle of the turf,' he said, 'lays it down that the best should win, and it may be that a Derby of the future might be run with a horse of Phar Lap's type standing in his box. What credit would accrue to the winner in such a year?'

Double trouble

The author D.H. Lawrence once remarked that in his view the most common characteristic of Australians was their 'indifference'. She'll be right, mate. But now, in so many ways, things weren't right. For many Australians, these were desperate times. As the unemployment queues grew longer and the economic headlines more depressing, and as Australians questioned their place in and value to the rest of the world, they turned to their heroes for reassurance. The champions became the standard bearers who would prove that Australia was okay. By the time of Bradman's twenty-second birthday, on 28 August 1930, 'Our' Don had been elevated to a hero status above any of the greats of the past. Through his daredevil exploits and helped by the publicity generated by the wonders of radio and instantly cabled photographs, Charles Kingsford Smith became the latest and greatest Australian airman, a more than worthy successor to Keith and Ross Smith and the much-lamented Bert Hinkler. 'Our' bridge, which climbed above and across 'our' harbour, was lauded by Sydneysiders as a unique technological advance. The working man yearned for another Les Darcy, the much revered young champion who'd died in America during the Great War, and saw in the promising welterweight Jack Carroll someone who just might be able to set the record straight for what the Yanks were rumoured to have done to poor Les.

And there was Phar Lap. The wonder-horse who didn't just win, but made hacks out of his rivals. Punters and non-punters alike knew his story and liked what they saw. Just as Bradman, the boy from Bowral, and Kingsford Smith, the Gallipoli veteran, were salt of the earth, so was Telford's champion. Bought for a song, trained by a battler, now capable of beating the world. Simple. Thus Phar Lap was given folk-hero status, elevated above almost all the champions of the Australian turf.

All but one. Still revered above all others was Carbine, 'Old Jack', the idol of the 1890s, when Australia was last in recession. Since then, all Australian racehorses had been compared unfavourably to Old Jack. Carbine had won the 1890 Cup carrying 10.5, and then gone to the old country to sire an English Derby winner. The wise old men of the turf shook their heads when younger fools suggested that horses such as Poseidon, Prince Foote, Poitrel, Windbag and Manfred might have beaten him. 'Ah, there'll never be another Carbine.'

'But what,' the children of the twentieth century would reply, 'what if Phar Lap wins the Cup with 9.12? Carbine didn't win the Cup as a four-year-old—he ran second with 10 stone. Surely, that would make our horse as good?'

AS SOON AS the Melbourne Cup weights came out on 1 July, a Melbourne bookmaker, who had never before opened his Cup market with the favourite as short as 6–1, was claimed for £6000 to £1000.

This would be the biggest straight-out bet he would hold on the champion until Cup Day itself, when he laid £5000 to £4000 just before the horse disappeared into odds-on. From day one, the Phar Lap/Phar Lap Caulfield Cup/Melbourne Cup double was extremely popular, as was Nightmarch/Phar Lap, Amounis/Phar Lap and Carradale/Phar Lap. But even at this stage, four months before the big race, it seemed that there were precious few chances, so the odds available weren't exorbitant. Even so, the bookies took on all comers, for they knew that many fancies in July never see the Cup start on the first Tuesday in November.

With Nightmarch having been given 9.11 in the Melbourne Cup, Phar Lap would meet him, if both horses started, 25 lb worse off for having been beaten convincingly in the 1929 race. Nightmarch had carried 9.2 in the '29 Cup, Phar Lap 7.6.

However, after the 1930 autumn racing, few gave Nightmarch a chance of beating the great chestnut champion again. This fact might have been on the mind of Mr Louisson, the owner of Nightmarch, when he candidly admitted that he was just as keen on the New Zealand Cup, to be run in early November, as he was on chasing a second Melbourne Cup. Shipping schedules meant that the horse could not run in the Melbourne Cup if he wanted to be in the prestigious New Zealand race. Meanwhile, in Melbourne, Carradale's owner, L.K.S. Mackinnon, was more concerned with reports that his big hope in July's VRC Grand National Steeple, Kentle, had been got at the night before the race by what one journalist called 'a gang of ruffians who will stop at nothing to carry out dastardly work in the nobbling of racehorses'. The gang, the report continued, had established a 'reign of terror', which left many racing people too frightened to come forward, 'for fear of what may happen to them'.

Normally, the nation stops for three minutes and around twenty-five seconds on the first Tuesday in November, for the Melbourne Cup. However, in 1930, in the weeks leading up to those three minutes and twenty-five seconds, because of Phar Lap—his unique ability, the awe in which he was regarded by so much of the battling community, and the mystery that invariably surrounded him—the nation would be involved for much, much longer. By the time Phar Lap stepped out for his first assignment as a four-year-old, in the Warwick Stakes at Warwick Farm on 30 August, the stage was already set for what would prove to be the most controversial and dramatic three months in the annals of the Australian turf.

> **Musket:** Why that 3lb allowance for geldings is still continued is hard to understand, for if Phar Lap were entire he would have 3lb more to carry and yet it is all of Sydney to an orange that he could give any stallion at present racing more than 3lb and a beating.

After the Warwick Stakes, poor Musket might have been arguing that because Amounis was a gelding he hadn't just tossed away the city for a piece of fruit. But the fact remained that Phar Lap had been beaten first-up again, and for the second campaign in a row, by the remarkable, now eight-year-old Amounis. Nightmarch was third, three lengths away from the first two, who had matched strides over the final furlong. The winner's time matched the track record. Immediately, Amounis swapped places with Nightmarch in the Caulfield Cup betting markets, right behind Phar Lap, while Jim Pike was obliged to counter criticism for what some thought was a rather sedate ride on his champion. 'I might have won with Phar Lap if I had sat up and flogged the horse home over the last furlong,' he responded after The Sun ran a lead story questioning his tactics. 'But would anybody ask a jockey to do that on a good plucky horse who was having his first run for five months? It's not sensible, and the thrashing might have settled him altogether.'

Frank McGrath, Amounis' wily trainer, immediately packed his bags for Melbourne, leaving Nightmarch and others in the beaten brigade, including Limerick, Chide, Loquacious and Fuji San, to contemplate tackling Phar Lap for the remainder of the Sydney spring.

Harry Telford: I was not disappointed at defeat, and certainly not surprised, considering it was only half a head that he went down to the best old horse in Australia, Amounis. Phar Lap is out of the paddock only six weeks. I did my best in that time to have him as near winning condition as possible, while at the same time keeping reserves for all the hard racing he has to go through in the remainder of his spring campaign.

Telford admitted to *The Daily Pictorial* that the Melbourne Cup was Phar Lap's mission, and that the major weight-for-age races in Sydney and Melbourne would be the 'stepping stones' to that great event. No mention was made of the Caulfield Cup. In fact, the doubts over Phar Lap and Nightmarch's spring engagements had all but stifled major Cups doubles betting. Most books reported that there had been good business done on the Amounis/Phar Lap double at reasonable odds, and some trade on the two Phar Laps at ridiculously cramped prices, but that was about it. Few thought Phar Lap would run in the Caulfield Cup, given that Telford had said the horse would run in the Randwick Plate on 11 October, just a week before the Caulfield race, and that to win at Caulfield would mean a probable 10 lb penalty for the Melbourne Cup, the race Telford wanted. But complicating the issue somewhat was the fact that Telford's lease ran out in February. Speculation was strong that David Davis would take the champion to another trainer—Randwick-based Chris O'Rourke, who was doing some work for the American entrepreneur, was mentioned in some circles. Telford had entered Phar Lap for the Perth Cup, to be run over the new year, and was said to be serious about taking the horse west. The haul to Western Australia would just about rule out an autumn campaign. If all or any of this was true, perhaps Telford would try to make as much money while the sun shone, which meant a Caulfield Cup and Melbourne Cup assault.

What Telford did not know was that Davis, in cahoots with Eric Connolly, had been backing the Amounis/Phar Lap double. Connolly, putting himself in Telford's shoes, thought there was no way he'd risk a weight penalty for the Melbourne Cup by running the champion at Caulfield. Feedback from Davis on what Telford was thinking reinforced this belief. Of course, Connolly always knew what Mr Louisson was contemplating, which was a straight choice between the Caulfield Cup and the New Zealand Cup, with a leaning towards going home. Pressmen, through their columns, begged Telford to make up his mind, for the public's sake, but he refused. 'Bugger 'em, the public don't pay for the upkeep of the stables. I'll decide when I want to,' he growled. Connolly, thinking he might have misjudged things, decided to save on the two Phar Laps double.

Jim Pike: As a two-year-old, he was all legs. At three, he was lean and tall, still. But at four his body had begun to grow and fill out round those long great legs of his that made him look so high. He improved with age in the matter of looks.

Phar Lap breezed through his Sydney commitments, earning Telford more than £4000 and Davis more than £2000 for five easy wins. Each time he was long odds-on, each time he won at least comfortably and for the first four races the second horse home was Nightmarch. The only time the Kiwi got close was in the Spring Stakes, but Tommy Woodcock later claimed that Pike was riding under instructions to keep the finish close (the final margin was half a length), in the hope that the connections might get a good price in the Craven Plate four days later. If this was true, it might have caught out Eric Connolly, who was seen vigorously backing Nightmarch in from 12s to 5–1. Connolly did have inside information about a change of riding tactics, but Phar Lap won by six lengths anyway, breaking the Australasian record for a mile and a quarter in the process. 'He has a tireless lope,' wrote Musket, 'which enables him to cover ground at a tremendous rate without any apparent effort.'

C.J. Graves: What could he have done if ridden out? It was a marvellous performance and proved to be, in fact, the greatest test he has had in a race of this kind. There were peculiar circumstances which contributed to this. Connections of Nightmarch, sick of seeing him try to beat Phar Lap from behind, determined to try new tactics. 'Could he beat Phar Lap by running him into the ground?' they wondered. So off they went hammer and tongs, together, from the rise of the barrier. By reason of this competition, they ran the first half mile in 48³/₄, the six furlongs in 1:13¹/₄, and the mile in 1:36¹/₄. The Randwick record for the mile is 1:36¹/₄.

'He'll win all he starts in you know,' Telford had said to Theodore Charles Trautwein, not long after he'd rejected an offer from Mr Trautwein, made at Rosehill on 20 September, of £10,000 for the remaining five months of the Phar Lap lease. Telford wanted £12,000, which, reporters calculated, was just about exactly as much as Phar Lap could win for the trainer before the lease ran out (assuming the horse missed the Caulfield Cup and didn't go to Perth). Trautwein, an extremely colourful racing identity, owner of some of Sydney's finest hotels, financier of some of racing's most successful plunges and rumoured to be a friend and associate of some of the city's leading underworld figures, refused to up his bid, so the horse stayed with Telford. It was, though, by any measure, an amazing offer.

When asked at that same meeting whether someone had made an offer for Telford's lease, David Davis replied angrily, 'No, that's tommy rot.' In fact, Telford hadn't got around to telling him. The lessor would find out about it in the papers.

WOULD HE RUN in the Caulfield Cup? One reporter offered an interesting angle on 24 September. Perhaps the bookies might make it interesting by offering the trainer a cash inducement to start the horse? This had been done before—one scribe has suggested this was why Telford waited so long to scratch his horse from the Adelaide Cup—and made sense from the bagmen's perspective as Phar Lap was far from their worst risk in the Caulfield Cup. And a penalty wouldn't make his Melbourne Cup any easier. 'The honour of training a Melbourne Cup winner may appeal to Telford,' Cliff Graves wrote in The Referee, 'but most owners and trainers are in racing for what they are likely to get from it. Therefore, if the Caulfield were made as monetarily attractive as the Melbourne Cup for Phar Lap's lessee, he might decide it was as well to have two strings to his bow.'

What was the truth behind Telford's refusal to announce his Caulfield Cup intentions clearly depended on what story you heard about his alliance with Davis. Legend has it that the Phar Lap camp wanted to scare Nightmarch back to New Zealand, to make their Amounis/Phar Lap double a sure thing. But Telford arranged Phar Lap's program and he wasn't in on the bet. From day one, Telford had kept Davis out of the loop when crafting Phar Lap's program. The previous year, Davis had backed his three-year-old at long odds to win the Melbourne Cup, negotiated to cancel the bet when Telford announced the horse wouldn't run, then watched embarrassed when the gelding went out an even-money favourite without him. The fact the horse lost was small compensation for Davis' loss of face. 'A story that relations between owner and trainer have, to put it mildly, become "strained",' wrote Graves on 1 October, 'is given full credence in inner turf circles ... Any difference between lessee and lessor might mean that when the lease ends, relations will be severed.'

The Perth trip, Telford said elsewhere, was definitely on provided the Western Australian Turf Club came to the party with expenses. There were three suitable weight-for-age races to be run there, worth in total £1500 to the winner, plus the £3000 Perth Cup over two miles. In regard to the Caulfield and Melbourne Cups, big and small punters alike, who'd risked their hard-earned cash on a variety of combinations, didn't have a clue what was going on.

The Daily Pictorial reported on 10 October that 'a prominent punter backed Phar Lap on behalf of the stable a few days ago for the Caulfield Cup'. The wager was large enough for the gelding to firm a full point in betting. The Sydney Sportsman drew a comparison with the Nightmarch switch in 1929, from the Metropolitan to the Epsom. Maybe Eric Connolly was behind it all? Meanwhile, the connections of Nightmarch discovered that if they wanted to compete in the 1930 New Zealand Cup on 8 November they needed to be on the Marama, which was leaving Sydney Harbour on 17 October, and that bookings needed to be confirmed a week before. No other ship could get them home in time. Final acceptances for the Caulfield Cup would be taken on 13 October, five days before the race.

Tommy Woodcock: The trainer of Nightmarch come to me down on the course after the Wednesday meeting and the Craven Plate [at Randwick on 8 October] and said, 'Is he gonna run in the Caulfield Cup, Tommy?'

'As far as I know he'll be running in the Caulfield Cup,' I said.

'I don't know for sure, but I think he's going home at the weekend to get ready for the Caulfield Cup.'

'Oh blast 'im!' he said. 'I'm sick of chasing him. I'll go home ...'

After Phar Lap won the Randwick Plate on Saturday 11 October, Tommy Woodcock went about preparing for the journey south, on a special 'horse train' which left Sydney's Central Station the following day. Well-wishers at the station would note how empty the train was, compared to previous years. Another indication of the trying times came with the release of the betting and attendance figures for the recent AJC carnival—crowds were down by 70,000, turnover down almost £100,000 on the previous year. By this time, Telford was already in Melbourne, as were Davis and Connolly, and, finally, on the Sunday, Davis and Telford got together to thrash everything out.

AT MIDDAY ON the Monday, Phar Lap was still being backed in the first leg of Cups doubles. The consensus was that he would start, that there was no way Telford would have kept him in the Caulfield Cup all this time to scratch him now. But at around 1 p.m. that's exactly what he did. Immediately, there was a rush to back Amounis, the new favourite, who firmed several points. Cragford, the AJC Metropolitan winner, was now second pick, but there was little depth in the field. The only risk, it seemed, was the weather, for Amounis couldn't handle the wet. On the Wednesday, he was scratched from his final lead-up, the Herbert Power Handicap, but fine skies on the Thursday and Friday would ensure he ran as a pronounced favourite.

At first, Telford blamed the scratching on the railways. The horse, he claimed, had been held up at Albury, on the NSW/Victoria border, which meant that he wouldn't arrive in Melbourne until late Tuesday, rather than Monday as first planned. The Victorian railways, how-ever, quickly denied there had been any fault on their part, a point Telford pathetically conceded the following day. Without doubt, Telford handled his subterfuge very badly, which did little for his public standing. Many years later, Woodcock admitted that Telford had wired him with instructions to keep the horse in Albury.

Davis, not to be outdone, told reporters he knew no reason why the horse should have been taken out of the Caulfield Cup. From New Zealand, McAulay, the trainer of Nightmarch, denied that the probable presence of Phar Lap in the Caulfield Cup had any influence on their decision to return home. He reiterated the stable's desire to win a New Zealand Cup. But the Australian press was livid, taking up the cause of punters and bookmakers alike who had been conned into believing Phar Lap would run. Nightmarch supporters had done their money. Phar Lap backers had done their money. The markets had been a joke, unless you were 'in the know'. From not long after the Melbourne Cup was first run in 1861, Cups doubles betting had become something of an institution in Australian racing. And Harry Telford, selfish bastard, had wrecked it for everyone.

But why? On the Wednesday, Telford spoke again to reporters.

My lease of Phar Lap is nearly up, he began, and I would rather hand him back to his owner in good condition and see him live to be like Amounis, even if it means being misunderstood by the public. Mr Davis and I considered it was asking too much of Phar Lap to expect him to win the Caulfield and Melbourne Cups, and we thought it better to give him a chance of winning the Melbourne Cup. There is no truth in the mischievous rumour that Mr Davis and I were on bad terms over Phar Lap, and that I was overworking the horse in the last stages of my lease. It did influence me, however, in the scratching of the gelding, because running him at Caulfield in the circumstances might have been regarded as vindictiveness.

There was no mention of why he had left it to the last possible half hour to scratch the horse. Truth described Telford as being 'more famous than popular'. Jim Pike, who had rejected the ride on Amounis, was as caught out as anyone. Subsequent events strongly suggest that Davis and Telford had come to an agreement that involved not only the 1930 Caulfield Cup but also Phar Lap's future racing career. Before the end of the week, Telford announced that the trip to Perth was off. 'Considering the long journey involved and the comparative smallness of the stakes, the risk of knocking the horse about would be too great,' he explained. Again, what had changed from two weeks earlier, when the trip was definitely on? Most likely, the answer would be revealed in mid-November, when David Davis registered some new colours with the AJC—red, red and green hooped sleeves, black cap. These were far removed from his usual silks—purple, white Maltese cross, orange cap—and much closer to Telford's red, black and white hooped sleeves and red cap. A little more than a month later, Telford travelled to Sydney to sign an agreement with Davis that gave him a half share in Phar Lap for £4000. From the expiry of the lease, the horse would run in Davis' new colours. Which begs the question—if Davis wouldn't give Telford the right to a half share around the time in early 1928 he refused to pay another cent on the horse's upkeep, why would he suddenly sell half a share in the horse of the century for 4000 quid just a few weeks after Telford had knocked back £10,000 for the last five months of the lease?

The Brisbane Courier-Mail's long-time racing writer, Bill Ahern, in his magnificent book on the Melbourne Cup, A Century of Winners, states that Telford did have a clause inserted in the original lease agreement, which allowed him to purchase a half share for £4000 if he so chose. However, this is the only reference to such a clause existing, and as we have seen others have contended that Davis scoffed at such a concept when Telford originally put it to him.

Perhaps Telford spun this line afterwards, to cover the true tale? Another story is that Mrs Davis insisted her husband offer Telford a 50/50 split, in gratitude for all he had done. But Davis was a hard-headed businessman—to him, offering to leave the horse in Telford's stables, with the trainer getting the customary trainer's percentage, would have been gratitude enough. Tommy Woodcock always contended that Telford had tricked Davis into thinking the horse was lame and thus a risky racing proposition, but he suggested this occurred in late February 1931, around the time of his own wedding, which was after the lease expired. Surely any negotiations would have been long completed by that point, a fact confirmed categorically in contemporary press reports. And anyway, David Davis was no mug. More likely is the scenario that Telford used the fact that Davis had a hefty Amounis/Phar Lap Cups double running, and the fact that if he wasn't kept on board he would run the horse in everything until the lease ran out, to lever the American into giving him a half share in the champion. Whether Telford was also cut in on the Cups double bounty is only conjecture. But until the deal was nutted out, Phar Lap stayed in the Caulfield Cup. Never mind the punters, the press, the clubs; Harry Telford was looking after himself.

TELFORD WAS KEEN to get out of the public eye, if only for a moment, and retreated to Braeside. There he supervised not only Phar Lap's work but also the rest of his big team, including a pair of two-year-olds of some promise, La Justice and Old Ming. One of his two track riders was another Telford apprentice with the surname of Martin—Jack—who was proving just about as capable as his little namesake from Kensington. However, Phar Lap's main accomplice on the training track was the sixteen-year-old Bobby Parker. Telford's intention was to give Phar Lap no more than a few days R&R at Braeside, before getting him back to Caulfield, to old Joe Cripps' stables where he'd been stationed twelve months before.

Amounis duly won the Caulfield Cup, beating the second smallest field in the race's history and leaving doubles bookmakers, especially those in Sydney, with a colossal headache after they calculated the extent of their liabilities. *The Referee* wrote immediately after the race that 'the total of all the big operators is £60,000 against the [Amounis/Phar Lap] combination', but in the days and years since estimates of the betting ring's liability have risen significantly higher. Certainly, the double had opened at 200–1 when weights were issued, and there were plenty of takers, most of them small investors, at that sort of price. By mid July, it had firmed to 110–1, and by mid-August was in as tight as 40–1. Precisely when Connolly and Davis backed the double is impossible to determine, but whenever it was, there is no doubt that many bookmakers would much rather Amounis had not won.

It must be stressed that while the bookies' liabilities were substantial they were not unprecedented. What had raised the ire of the racing fraternity, and some shadowy types on racing's periphery, was the apparently devious manner in which the sting was stung.

The Arrow (24 October 1930): That there are influences at work, however, which would bring about a forced scratching if possible is apparent from an incident reported on Wednesday. When Phar Lap was exercising on the roads a car charged straight at him and he only swerved in time to escape injury. It was thought at first to be a drunken escapade, then carelessness. But when a bystander noticed that the number plate had been covered with brown paper, it put a sinister aspect on the incident, making it evident that a deliberate attempt had been made to maim the Cup favourite.

It was clearly schemed in accordance with the deepest plots of

American gunmen novels, and if achieved might have been mistaken for a hit-run accident.

The utmost precautions are now taken with Phar Lap. There are never less than three guarding him day and night and a bodyguard accompanies him in all his travels abroad, as was the case last year. It is probably as well that whenever he goes to race meetings he will be conveyed by float with the greatest care to avoid traffic jams and possible interference. Moreover, he will again wear that peculiar head piece that made him look like an old grandmother with spectacles on, designed with mica-covered holes to safeguard him against the throwing of corrosive acid.

Apparently there is at work in Victoria a gang which specialises in the putting of favourites out of notable events . . .

When pressed on this incident, Telford told reporters he knew nothing about it. Which, given Telford's prevailing attitude to the press, meant it may or may not have happened.

On the Saturday after the Caulfield Cup, Phar Lap went to Moonee Valley to be booed by punters still seething over his late Caulfield Cup scratching and to win the W.S. Cox Plate easily from the AJC Derby winner Tregilla and the venerable Mollison. Tregilla's was an interesting tale—the colt's nomination for the Victoria Derby had been refused by the VRC the year before, when entries closed, because he was owned by the wife of a trainer, and that was against the club's sometimes bizarre and archaic rules. However, by the time for Melbourne Cup entries the ownership had been transferred to Mrs Battye's husband, Cecil, so the horse was allowed to compete in the Cup, and was now seen as one of Phar Lap's biggest dangers. Tregilla would meet Phar Lap 20 lb better in the Cup for being beaten by three lengths in the Cox Plate, and like Phar Lap would have his final preparatory run for the big race in the Melbourne Stakes on Derby Day.

Telford tried to keep as low a profile as possible, a feat he managed despite his horse being the lead story on the racing pages from Monday through to Sunday. By this point, Telford was questioning whether winning the Melbourne Cup was worth all the heartache. He hated being painted as some sort of crook by the press, even though he knew that much of it was his own making. No-one had trained him for being so much in the public eye. And now, every time the phone rang, he froze for a moment, assuming it was either another reporter searching for an angle or another crank ready to tell him what he was going to do to the horse. The trainer didn't know it, but Davis, Pike and Woodcock had been copping crank calls as well. He did know that these bastards on the line sounded fair dinkum. All the time, night and day, there was a villain lurking behind the next fence, waiting behind the next tree, hidden in the bloody shadows. But they all got through the week, somehow.

The Shooting

At about 5.45 a.m., as Woodcock, the pony and Phar Lap approached the car, Woodcock noticed the rear registration plate with rough, whitewashed numbers. Inside were a driver and a rear-seat passenger, each with his face buried in a newspaper. Alerted to dire consequences and expecting them at any moment, Woodcock led his companions south across Glenhuntly Road and into James Street. As he did, he heard the car grumble into life behind him. He urged the pony and Phar Lap into a trot and turned right into Etna Street, forty metres along James Street. He tested the side gate of the corner house in a vain attempt to get Phar Lap off the street. As the car crossed Glenhuntly Road, the driver began sounding the horn then sped into Etna Street, where Woodcock had Phar Lap against the fence on the right of the street, the pony and himself between Phar Lap and the car. The sounding horn caused Phar Lap to rear and twist, landing to face back the way they had just come. The car continued past Woodcock and a shotgun protruded from the back window. Woodcock kicked the pony and the sudden movement caused Phar Lap to move forward, increasing the distance between him and the still-moving car. A single shot rang out, and Phar Lap dragged Woodcock from the pony and back along the road towards James Street. The vehicle turned right at the other end of Etna Street and was later seen making haste towards the west along Glenhuntly Road ...

Dawn comes slowly during November in Melbourne. First light is half an hour before sunrise, which was at 5.14 a.m. that Saturday morning. The streets on the south side of Caulfield racecourse are residential but dotted with racing stables. Trainers live in the house facing the street and the backyard is a roof over half a dozen loose boxes. Families of four next to four-legged athletes.

Beverley Street in Glenhuntly is a short land-locked avenue, 600 metres south of the back gate of the racecourse. In 1930 on the western end stood Joe Cripps' stables. Phar Lap was stabled there for the spring carnival. Tommy Woodcock slept in the horse's box and rode a grey pony to lead him to early work at the Caulfield course.

Phar Lap cantered a gentle two furlongs on the sand as a stretch for the Melbourne Stakes in which he was running at Flemington later that day. Woodcock rugged the champion and, despite apprentice Bobby Parker asking him to wait so Parker could help out with the two horses, set off for Cripps' stables.

The back gate of the course opens on to Neerim Road, running east–west. Manchester Grove is perpendicular to Neerim Road and directly opposite the gate. With a direct line of sight down Manchester Grove to Glenhuntly Road, across it into James Street and on to the eastern end of Beverley Street, Manchester Grove was the quickest way home for Woodcock and Phar Lap. It was also the most obvious place to hole up for an ambush.

Horses wearing rugs were travelling in all directions. Six hundred horses were trained at Caulfield at that time and the toing and froing from the back gate of the course was continuous. Phar Lap was rugged and wearing his bandages on his front legs. The light at 5.30 in the morning was grey but clear. To distinguish a racehorse from hundreds of others required both a close inspection and a prior knowledge.

Manchester Grove is long and straight and bare. As Woodcock led Phar Lap towards Glenhuntly Road he noticed a car parked outside the cinema at the intersection. Cars were not common enough to be part of the background in 1930. A car parked in a side street before six o'clock in the morning, with two occupants hiding behind newspapers, was like a beacon in a fog. James Creed, *The Sun News-Pictorial* racing representative, saw the car on his way to the track at 5.10 a.m. and noted the car's front registration number. It was not the same number that Woodcock noted on the rear. Joe Bird, a trainer with stables in Manchester Grove, also saw the vehicle.

Woodcock and Telford claim to have received threatening letters in the weeks leading to the Melbourne Cup. Poison darts, needles, hit and run accidents and bullets had all been suggested as ways in which Phar Lap would be prevented from winning the Cup. Expecting an attempt on the horse's health, if not his life, Woodcock had asked Telford to send a stable pony up from Braeside in Mentone because, as he put it, 'I can get home quicker on a pony than what I can running with him.'

AFTER THE SHOOTING, the pony was retrieved and brought to Woodcock by a milkman doing his rounds in Etna Street, and Woodcock took Phar Lap back to Cripps' stables. One of the stable boys was sent to find Telford, still on the racecourse, to tell him the big horse had been shot at.

The shooting was a sensation in Melbourne. The racing world was abuzz. Newspapers ran headlines such as 'DASTARDLY ATTEMPT TO MAIM CUP FAVOURITE'. And it was news outside the sporting world: the *Herald* ran front-page stories on the afternoon of the shooting and another front-page story the following Monday. False reports were phoned to police and the media that Phar Lap had been poisoned and his stables bombed.

At Flemington, the Derby Day racing took second place in conversations to the attempt on Phar Lap's life. The motorfloat which took the champion to Flemington was preceded by an unmarked police car containing two detectives, and was followed by two motorcycle police. During the procession of runners before the Melbourne Stakes, Phar Lap was escorted into the mounting yard by two policemen, who did not leave his side until he was safely on the course proper. They were at the gate to meet him on his return after an effortless victory.

THERE IS SPECULATION about the target of the shot. Woodcock said he thought the gun was aimed at Phar Lap's legs. With eight legs to hit, the Sydney *Truth* of Sunday 2 November, sums up the situation best:

> With dramatic suddenness it was announced that two men had waylaid the champion in a blue sedan car; that a double-barrelled shot-gun had been pointed at him; and that a man in the back seat had fired—from across the street—and missed!
>
> Apart altogether from the question of marksmanship, Melbourne, and all Australia, is intrigued to know exactly what is behind the sensational incident.

Questions about marksmanship indeed. There is a more fundamental question: was the gun loaded? *Truth* made a great deal of the fact that no shotgun pellets were found. In a report headed 'From "Truth" Special Representative, Melbourne, Saturday Night', a number of claims were made:

> The failure of the police investigating the Phar Lap affair to find any pellets, lends colour to the theory that the gun may have held a blank and that the miscreants' intention was not to wound or kill the horse, but to frighten him in the hope that he would break away and injure himself sufficiently to prevent his running in the Cup.

A search was made today for pellets, but not even a mark of one was found . . .

Meanwhile, half a dozen different stories had been broadcast. One racing sheet came out with a special edition in which it was stated that three shots had been fired and that the rugs covering Phar Lap had been penetrated.

The police denied this, however, and say that their investigations led them to believe that only one shot was fired.

They consider also that a very light charge of shot must have been used in the gun, the idea being to merely pepper the horse's legs in such fashion that he would not be permanently disabled but would be prevented from keeping his engagements at Flemington.

This report raises some questions, but as it had Phar Lap being led by 'Trevor' Woodcock back to Joe Bird's stables in Manchester Grove, it should be treated with caution.

Melbourne's Saturday evening *Herald* covered the incident as a front-page story. Eyewitness accounts were given and a photographic recreation of the scene was published. Norman Taylor, a fourteen-year-old newsboy, was delivering papers in James Street at the time. He heard the shot fired but did not see the gun. Mr F. Bayley, a resident of James Street, said he heard the shot and 'was certain it was a gunshot and not the backfiring of a car'.

The Argus dealt with the incident on Monday, 3 November. In part, the report read:

A theory in some quarters that the incident was a stunt and that a blank cartridge was fired was disproved when Mr J. Bird, racehorse trainer of Manchester Grove Caulfield, found near the fence against which Phar Lap had been led, the cardboard wad from the cartridge. On it were marks made by the leaden pellets. Mr Bird made a mark

on the fence near where he found the wad. He was unable to find
any pellets or any marks where pellets had struck the fence. Yesterday
morning, however, Mr W.J. Hall of Queens Avenue, Caufield, the
track representative of 'The Argus', found several No.6 pellets on
the footpath about 6 yards nearer James Street and others were
found embedded in the fence. The angle at which they had entered
the wood proved that the motorcar had passed Phar Lap when
the occupant of the rear seat fired at him through the window.
Detective Sergeant Brophy found at the same place a piece of
newspaper riddled with pellets. The distance between the holes
indicated that the charge had travelled about 20 yards. Some of the
marks on the fence were about 2 feet from the ground and others
about 3 feet.

The Age reported on the same day that:

Definite evidence of the attempted shooting was obtained by
Detective Sergeant Brophy and Detective H.G. Saker when they made
a search of the scene of the outrage yesterday (Sunday) morning.
Embedded in a cypress tree, they recovered two shotgun pellets. Five
pellets and a cartridge case cap were found on the footpath close to
the fence. The detectives expressed the opinion that the charge was
fired about three feet six inches off the ground and at an angle of
45 degrees (to the fence). The object of the men, they said, was to
wound Phar Lap in the flanks and so injure him that he would have to
be withdrawn from the Melbourne Cup.

At the time of the shooting, statements were taken from witnesses
by Senior Constable Davis of Glenhuntly. There are no reports of a
search being made by him, but by Saturday afternoon Detectives
Brophy and Saker were in charge of the investigation and according

to The Argus, 'met the float [carrying Phar Lap] at the course and Phar Lap was guarded by ten police in uniform until his stall was reached'.

It was not until Sunday morning that the detectives searched the scene of the crime.

WHILE AT FLEMINGTON on the day of the shooting, Harry Telford sought the assistance of Mr Guy Raymond, a VRC committeeman and owner of St Albans, an 800-acre stud near Geelong. The generally secretive Telford had now to contend with an unknown, uncontrollable, external influence on how he prepared his horse. He resorted to the tactic he had used many times before: subterfuge.

At about 1.30 a.m. on Sunday morning, Tommy Woodcock laid mats and empty bags on the concrete outside Phar Lap's box. In a borrowed rug, the champion was led onto a motorfloat driven by Stan Boyden, the trainer's usual carrier, who had been asked to report to Cripps' stables, task and destination unknown. Once the horse and the two-year-old La Justice, which had won the Maribyrnong Plate for Telford at Flemington on Derby Day, were loaded, the driver was told to head for Raymond's St Albans stud, about 70 kilometres south of Melbourne.

A few hours later, the party was sleeping uneasily in their new campaign headquarters, Telford having left the care of the horse to Woodcock and Raymond, hardly his original plan to have Phar Lap primed for the most important race of his career. Sunday was spent walking the paddocks of the stud among the ghosts of Wakeful, Briseis (which won the Derby, the Oaks and the Melbourne Cup in 1876) and Mersey (the dam of the great Carbine, and thus an ancestor of Phar Lap).

That night, electricity and telephone connections were cut during a storm. Feeling the weight of Telford's trust, Raymond rushed into

Geelong to recruit two friends to stand armed guard over Phar Lap. Meanwhile in Melbourne Jim Pike shut himself away and Telford continued to exercise his horses at Caulfield. A large two-year-old chestnut, Old Ming, was asked to act as Phar Lap's body double and wearing Phar Lap's bandages and rugs was transported by float with police guard to Caulfield. It worked in front of a largely unknowing crowd at morning trackwork. There is no record of the unfortunate asked to be Woodcock's impersonator.

On Monday, Phar Lap was walked by back lanes to the Geelong racecourse and given some light work by his usual track rider, Bobby Parker, who had travelled to St Albans with Woodcock. On Cup morning he ran three furlongs at the course in 37 seconds and Guy Raymond's stand-in role was completed.

The drama was not. As the motorfloat arrived to transport Phar Lap to Flemington, so did the rain. After loading the horse, the waterlogged engine would not start and the police escorts—two to ride in the float and two motorcyclists—took turns winding the crank handle. Time ticked away but the engine would not. After what seemed an age, the engine sparked and the motorfloat raced up the Melbourne Road, arriving at the course just as the race before the Cup was being run.

THERE ARE FEW unarguable facts about the attempted assassination of Phar Lap. That Woodcock showed exemplary bravery is one of them. He did not know what form the attack on Phar Lap was to take, yet he knowingly put his body between the car and his horse. Reports published since suggest that not only did he put himself in the line of fire but he watched as the shotgun was fired long enough to know that the gunman's aim was low and to see the handkerchief disguise fall from the gunman's face.

The physical evidence of the shooting is at best mysterious. On Monday 3 November *The Herald* had on its front page a photograph showing a 10-centimetre-square piece of fence with three pellets in it. On Saturday, there had been no pellets, no evidence of pellets and no piece of pellet-riddled newspaper. On Sunday morning, more than twenty-four hours after the incident, somewhere between ten and fifteen pellets were found, some in the fence, five on the footpath and two in the tree above the 175-centimetre fence.

According to Senior Constable Ray Vincent, a ballistics expert from the Victorian Forensic Centre in January 2000, a shotgun firing a cartridge of No. 6 pellets at a fence from 20 metres and at an angle of 45° will leave an elliptical shot pattern approximately 50 centimetres wide in its narrower dimension. And it would leave 270 to 300 pellets in the fence. A blast fired straight at the fence would leave a circular pattern 34–45 centimetres in diameter. The size of the shot pattern depends upon the length and choke of the barrel of the shotgun.

A 'blank' charge can be made by packing a used cartridge case with gunpowder and a second-hand cardboard wad. The wad found by Bird and the absence of pellets of any description on Saturday and the presence of so few on Sunday, indicate that the shot was a blank. It seems reasonable to also draw the conclusion that pellets and a 'pellet-riddled' piece of newspaper were left at the scene after the event, probably on Saturday night.

WHY DID THE TWO MEN in the car try to stop Phar Lap? The punt was important in those Depression days of 1930. Huge money would be taken from the bookies' ring if Phar Lap won the Cup. Hoodlums in dark cars putting the slows on the bookies' nightmare has always been a popular explanation for the gunfire in Glenhuntly.

Supporters of this theory argue that doubles bookmakers had two possible strategies. One was to injure Phar Lap so he would be scratched, or to make Telford or Davis so concerned about his safety that he would be withdrawn to keep him alive, thus ensuring significant winnings to all bookmakers. The other was to deceive fellow bookies. By making the attempt look serious, even though it wasn't, it is possible that another horse, perhaps Tregilla, would become more favoured. The bookmaker in the know could hope that the drama and secrecy around Phar Lap's preparation would cause easing in his odds and let the mastermind lay off his Phar Lap liability at better odds. Both strategies seem complicated, and the motive was not as strong as is popularly believed. Despite reports to the contrary, the losses faced by the bookies in the event of a Phar Lap victory were by no means the largest seen in the previous few years.

Warning or spectacle? In 1932, an article about Phar Lap's attempt on the 1931 Melbourne Cup was printed in *The Bloodhorse Breeders' Review*, a conservative publication from the United Kingdom. It contained the following:

In the story we wrote about last year's Melbourne Cup, mention is made of the report that, early in the morning of the day Phar Lap won the Melbourne Stakes a shot was fired at him (without effect) while he was returning to his stable from the training ground at Caulfield. The news created a tremendous sensation. It was stated that the man with the gun was in a motor car 'which disappeared from the scene of the outrage at top speed, and the miscreant was not discovered'. And no wonder, for, according to a letter we have received from a friend well known in Melbourne press circles, 'the story was jokingly concocted by three journalists on the Thursday before Derby day.' It had, our informant states, been planned to hoax the public with another dreadful tale this year—a tale in which a poisoned dart was to figure prominently, but the scheme fell through. Perhaps those associated with Phar Lap had heard of the phantom dart, and so provided the horse with a formidable escort when he appeared on the racetrack. We gather that the conspiring journalists were animated by an irresistible desire to make fun of the 'Phar Lap hysteria' with which Australians had become afflicted.

Much of the conjecture about the shooting seems to ignore a number of issues. Tommy Woodcock was in the line of fire when the gun was discharged. If the police thought the pellets were real, why was there no investigation into the attempted murder? Newspapers worked hard to give the impression that the police thought little harm was intended and the episode was an attempt to scare Phar Lap so that he would bolt and injure himself. Why would hoodlums return to the scene to plant evidence of a serious attempt at injury? If a low shot at the horse's legs was intended, why was the car horn sounded? If the report in The Bloodhorse Breeders' Review can be believed, the whole incident was a stunt.

THE IDENTITY AND MOTIVE of the two men in the dark-coloured Studebaker with the falsified number plates remain unknown. What is absolutely certain is that the 'shooting' and its aftermath would have crippled the Melbourne Cup campaign of a lesser horse.

Wonderful what a horse can do

The Australasian (1 November 1930): The Melbourne Cup was established in 1861. The increase in the value of the prize was gradual until the added money reached £10,000 in 1890. In spite of the comparatively small stakes attached to the early Cups the race caught the fancy of owners and the public. It became a great betting event, and that no doubt had much to do in establishing the race in popular favour ...

When Mentor won the Melbourne Cup in 1888 the attendance was supposed to have reached 150,000, but that was probably an exaggeration, because Flemington in those days was not so well equipped as it is today and it would be almost impossible to accommodate a crowd of that size under existing conditions. It is certain that the accommodation on Melbourne Cup day this year will not be overtaxed because, although the meeting attracts people from all ports of Australia, there is likely to be a serious decline in the attendance. There was a falling off of 33 per cent at the recent AJC meeting and the drop was nearly as great at the Caulfield Cup meeting. There is no reason to believe that the VRC will fare any better than the other clubs ...

Bookmakers, confused by the various reports as to what might have happened at Caulfield on the morning of the Melbourne Stakes but knowing what they'd seen in the afternoon—Phar Lap easily beating Tregilla and Amounis—saw no reason to ease the favourite's Melbourne Cup quote. This was even though some students of racing history pointed out that only the sport's greatest legend, Carbine in 1890, and its most versatile champion, Malua (who won a two-mile Melbourne Cup, a six-furlong Newmarket, a five-and-a-half furlong Oakleigh Plate and a three-mile Grand National Hurdle during his unique career) in 1884, had ever successfully completed the Melbourne Stakes/Melbourne Cup double in the same year.

> **Harry Telford (on the Monday):** Phar Lap will win the Melbourne
> Cup without effort. Some people who know that he is a good thing
> for the race have become desperate in their attempt to prevent him
> from getting to the post. The public can be assured that I will take no
> risk of anyone doing damage to the horse between now and the time
> that he steps on the course at Flemington.

For a moment, Melbourne was distracted by the presence of Don Bradman, enjoying a triumphal journey across Australia after smashing record after record on Australia's recent tour of England. Over 5000 supporters, all grateful for the way he had so gallantly and conclusively belted the Poms, waited for more than two hours at Essendon Airport on the Sunday evening, just to catch of glimpse of their hero. Bradman was greeted by the former Australian captains, Warwick Armstrong and Jack Ryder, before being escorted by troopers into town for a civic reception and the first of a series of media commitments, including a live broadcast on Radio 3DB, organised for him by his new sponsors. Fans lined his route into the city. The feature of the following day was a big function at the Tivoli

Theatre, before he headed back to Essendon to board the *Southern Cloud*, for a flight to his home town of Bowral. There he would be wildly welcomed by yet another adoring crowd and, one presumes, would also listen to Tuesday's Melbourne Cup on the radio.

On the same Monday that Bradman was at the Tivoli, Phar Lap was being exercised at the Geelong racecourse, located about 1½ kilometres from St Albans.

In Sydney, *Sydney Sportsman*'s editor, A.B. 'Banjo' Paterson, set about writing the editorial for the paper's special Cup edition.

A.B. Paterson: The first Tuesday in November, today's the day. This means far more to Australians, today, than any balancing of budgets, results of Imperial Conferences or the price of duck eggs in Honolulu. It's Melbourne Cup day. All eyes will be focused on Flemington, irrespective of whether those eyes are located in the Cape York Peninsula or way out west in Broome, where they lower the sun with a windlass ...

How many Australians will refrain from having a bet on the Cup today? Only a very small minority. The big majority of people in this country, including very many who never see the inside of a racecourse, will have a go. The preponderance will go for Phar Lap ... but all the people won't go for the favourite. There are 16 others in the field and irrespective of their chances on form they will meet with support. Some because they will sport certain colours, others because someone has dreamt that they will prove the winner.

The Cup is the greatest race south of the Line ... even if the attendance is smaller today, interest is no less than it was last year. Those who cannot make the trip to Flemington will be there in spirit and a big percentage will be listening in on the wireless, to 'see' how the race is won ...

Many Phar Lap backers are fearful that the money interests

involved—he represents a liability of over half a million to the bookmakers—will prove a stumbling block to his success. In the circumstances, it behoves the stipendiary stewards to see that nothing of an untoward nature happens to Phar Lap.

If he is good enough, let him win. And if it is a clearly run race he should win and hearten the thousands of backers who will have their money on him in today's great race.

CUP MORNING WAS WET and bookmakers praying for an outsider's Cup tried to convince themselves that this made Phar Lap's task harder still. But the favourite's record on slow tracks was outstanding—it seemed all surfaces came alike to him. Meanwhile, society's finest were dreading what the weather might do to their outfits, while men whose businesses were struggling were happier for a moment because they now had an excuse for again wearing last year's suit.

During the parade in the mounting yard, Phar Lap was shadowed closely by two policemen, one on each side of the chestnut. 'There really was no need for this theatrical display,' recalled Samuel Griffiths, sports editor of The Australasian, three years later. 'Had anyone made the slightest attempt to injure the favourite, the crowd would have torn them to pieces.' As the horses paraded out down the straight it was noticed that while Phar Lap was first out onto the course, befitting the racebook order, Pike was in no hurry to get to the start. 'The champion,' wrote the Argus the following day, 'followed the others at a long interval.' The experienced horseman was giving the champion every chance to find his feet. While word had spread like wildfire on course that Phar Lap had not arrived until just after 2.30 p.m., less than an hour before the jump, very few knew of the drama that had occurred on the favourite's eventful journey from Geelong to the track.

Jim Pike: I was waiting on the course that day and usually I don't get on my toes, no matter how great the occasion might be, but this day I was definitely. The horse hadn't come. I knew everybody was on tenterhooks, but he wouldn't come early. But when the hour of the Cup approached and he still hadn't turned up, I began to think those threats had come true.

About two minutes remained before weighing out for the Cup, when Harry came rushing in, and then I heard the story of how the float had broken down on the road from Geelong, miles out of Melbourne, with no phone, no other conveyance, nothing at all to help, the Cup favourite was marooned . . .

He got to the course, a blacksmith whisked off his shoes and plated him, he trotted and cantered to the weighing yard, I was rushed about like a taxi, and then we set out for the post. He never had a breather, or time to look around.

An average horse would have succumbed without a fight. But old Phar Lap won that Cup in a dog-trot . . .

In the crowd at Flemington on Cup Day 1930 was a young British sports writer, Denzil Batchelor, who had driven south from Sydney to experience the great race. In 1949, in a story entitled 'Horse of the Century', Batchelor remembered that journey, and especially the sight—too often on the 1000 km coast road—of desperate men stumbling south, heels long gone from their shoes, seeking escape from the indignity of the depression in Sydney, knowing full well that Melbourne offered nothing new. 'They knew hunger and hopelessness were over the next horizon, as behind the last,' he recalled.

Of the scene at the course on this first Tuesday in November, Batchelor wrote, 'Rain storm after rain storm crashed over the course. Then, with the famous lawns resembling a tank-churned battlefield of the Hindenburg line, the sun came royally out of the cloud-rack, the skies were washed over in April's tenderest water-colours, and the horses pranced and stretched and tip-toed in the grand parade . . .'

Denzil Batchelor: And then, with the whole ring roaring they'd take 11 to 8 Phar Lap or give 5–1 Tregilla, the 15 runners burst from the gate, a tumble of jewelled jackets and shimmering coats on the first leg from the tiger country to the course proper. Temptation cut loose into the lead, with Shadow King and the great Tregilla stretching out at his shoulder, and First Acre and Carradale nose to nose half a length back. Into the course they wheeled. It was still Temptation: hanging on to the lead like a good 'un—going away from his field. Now Muratti came at him, but the jockey's urging forearms plucked him forward. You could see daylight between Temptation and the next horse as they thundered past the judge's box on the first time round. Behind him, the field bunched. Muratti and Carradale showed in the van; Star God (with 'Togo' Johnstone up), First Acre and Soulton swinging round the first bend within striking distance—and the pace not yet on.

There they went to the milepost. Half the race behind them now, and Temptation two—three—four lengths clear!

'Stay like that, you beaut,' prayed a collarless figure beside me, too thin to be a windbreak, with bare ankles showing above his gym shoes. Now you could see them spinning away down the back straight: moving so slowly, far away, almost out of mind. Temptation first still, but was he going back to his field, or was the angle shifting as the horses foreshortened, slanting up the bend that straightened to the long run-in?

And now—with the world at last suspecting that he was to win his Cup from first stride to finish, with the lightning speed of the climax of a conjuring trick, Temptation disappeared out of the race. It was as sudden as that. Just as in the blink of an eye the vanishing lady is out of this world, so Temptation disappeared into thin air. The next moment every expert's eye was fixed unwinking on the red jacket with the black and white hooped sleeves behind. Here was Pike on Phar Lap coming through in the centre, at the moment of unwinding his invincible run.

The mind rushed back across the years. All this had happened before—in an earlier race for the Cup, for this was Pike's 14th cut at the prize which was yet to be his. Just so, years back, had he found himself forced to cut out the pace on Pantheon when Comus had folded up like a jackknife as the field straightened for the last gruelling half-mile. The effort had been forced on him too early then; Pantheon had faltered and stopped under him. Would it be that way again? Nine stone 12—on this cloying, whipped-chocolate track. Surely history was about to repeat itself.

And then Phar Lap came through the bunching field at the three furlongs. His great, prancing mechanical stride was balanced and unforced. There was one heartstopping moment when it seemed he was crossed and must check; but he drove through, without fuss or hurry, and straightened, well placed by the rails, and so stretched out on the long pull for home.

Only once now did there come a moment of drama. Tregilla, the Derby winner, dashed at him when they were halfway up the straight ... There was a flurry of whips, a lifting with spur and heel: and then the effort died away.

Phar Lap sailed home. His knees brushed his nose; he moved like a pitching ship. He came home, ahead by three huge, unbridgeable lengths—three lengths that divided not winner from second, but immortal from mortal. He won with his ears cocked. Behind him was little Lewis flailing Second Wind; while three-quarters of a length back Tehan on Shadow King just headed Donald out of third place ...

It was Jim Pike's first Melbourne Cup victory, at the fourteenth attempt, and the big crowd cheered him and his great horse from well before the furlong, when they realised the race was won, until long after he'd returned to scale. Pike's first Cup ride had been on a horse called Bobby, in Lord Nolan's year, back in 1908. Without a grin, he told reporters after the race that he was sorry nothing had come after him, to make a race of it. 'I believe,' he said, 'if there had been opposition, he could have done better than he did.'

TELFORD WAS AS ANIMATED and happy as anyone had ever seen him, and managed to thank everyone involved with the horse ... except David Davis. 'What can I say,' he began, when surrounded by pressmen, 'Phar Lap is a great horse. That seems to cover it.' He shaped to walk away, then continued, 'Naturally, I am more than proud to have won the Melbourne Cup with a horse which I picked out at a sale and which was sold for 160 guineas. Everyone's been mighty good to me. I feel that I cannot sufficiently thank all those who have assisted me to guard my horse since the dastardly attempt to shoot him. This includes the detectives and the police, T. Woodcock, his groom, Mr Raymond at St Albans, and S. Boyden, who had charge of the transport arrangements. My thanks are also due to Pike, for the splendid race he rode.' Interview over, Telford began to walk back towards his Cup winner. But Cliff Graves grabbed him and shook his hand. 'In the old days,' the former battler whispered to the journalist, 'nobody cared whether I was alive or dead. Wonderful what a good horse can do.'

David Davis, when the reporters finally reached him, graciously gave full credit to Telford and Pike. 'I never had a doubt the horse would succeed,' he commented, 'if given anything like a good run.' When asked about the future, he said flatly, 'Though his lease expires in February, I dare say the horse will never be separated from Telford.'

After the presentation, Telford's steely demeanour finally broke. While gripping the gold trophy in one hand, he held his son proudly aloft with the other. Still, the punters saw only a hint of a smile. As Telford followed Tommy Woodcock and his champion down to the birdcage, he nodded his head and stopped occasionally to politely acknowledge the well-wishers. At his stall he stood silently, once or twice giving Woodcock a hand. By this time a huge crowd had gathered to see the Cup winner cool down. Telford turned to them, mostly struggling battlers as he had once been and in many ways still was. Then he put his hand deep inside his trouser pocket, pulled out a wad of pound notes, waved them high as a symbol of triumph and then, grinning broadly, tossed them into the throng.

W. J. Stewart McKay: Watching Phar Lap win his Melbourne Cup, it was wonderful to see that, in spite of his immense weight (9.12), he was able to leave his field two furlongs from home and, going right away without effort, he won by three lengths. Such was the superb strength of the great stayer's heart that when he pulled up he walked to the winner's enclosure without the slightest sign of distress, and there was very little evidence of sweating when the saddle was removed. Few four-year-olds that have ever lived could have equalled this great handicap performance; but it must not be forgotten that Phar Lap had reached a degree in the evolution of staying power that few other horses have ever approached.

Despite the slow track, Phar Lap's time for the last half mile was 49 seconds, which equalled Artilleryman's 1919 time as the second-fastest final four furlongs in Cup history. Only Nightmarch had come home faster. Phar Lap smashed the weight-carrying record for a four-year-old, previously held by Nightmarch and Windbag (1925) at 9.2. He was only the second four-year-old gelding to win the race, after Haricot, who carried 6.7 to victory in 1874, and the first horse to start odds-on, at 11–8 on.

The following day, speculation was rife as to just how much money was taken out of the ring. One bookmaker confessed grimly he was unable to settle. Most, though, while admitting to losing heavily, suggested they'd seen worse days. The fact that books were still taking substantial bets on the favourite all the way to the jump, albeit at very skinny odds, indicated that a Phar Lap victory wasn't going to break them. The general consensus in Melbourne was that a Phar Lap win twelve months earlier would have been a worse result. The Australasian suggested the books' losses would run to about half that won by the supporters of the aptly named Revenue when that horse won the Cup in 1901. In Sydney, doubles operators admitted that while the payout would be huge it was nothing compared to the 1927 Epsom/Metropolitan double, when Eric Connolly master-minded a colossal sting. But the facts did not stop stories of bankruptcies circulating, which The Arrow's correspondent blamed on the fact that 'some bookmakers love to tell of their alleged heavy losses to any willing listener'.

The Referee mounted a special investigation, and discovered that 'winnings over Amounis and Phar Lap were thoroughly distributed throughout Australia in small parcels'. All up, the paper concluded, the result was an overall loss to the bookmaking fraternity of well over £100,000, with upwards of £200,000 being paid out after Phar Lap's win. David Davis was one of the biggest individual straight-out winners, having had £5000 to £1000 with Jim Hackett's bookmaking firm not long after the weights were issued. But this was small fry compared to Maude Vandenburg, who had won £20,000 on the double, plus more from straight-out bets on her favourite, Amounis, in the Caulfield Cup. Not that this was the full extent of their winnings. Connolly was rumoured to have collected £80,000 on the double, at average odds of 40–1, for a syndicate that included Vandenburg and Davis. However, Connolly had personally saved on the two Phar Laps double when it seemed Telford was going to run at Caulfield.

TELFORD HAD RESOLVED that if the horse pulled up well after the Cup, he would run again on the Thursday, in the weight-for-age Linlithgow Stakes, over a mile, and then on the Saturday in the mile-and-a-half C.B. Fisher Plate. He must have been both exasperated and amused when, in some quarters, he was criticised for asking too much of his horse, while others argued that Phar Lap couldn't be compared to Carbine because the champion of the previous Depression used to win two races on one day. Still, the two victories won another £2000, and did Phar Lap no harm. Or so it seemed.

On the same day Phar Lap won the Fisher Plate, his old foe Nightmarch was winning the New Zealand Cup at Canterbury, carrying 9.6. One reporter suggested that this win proved that Nightmarch was 'as good as at any previous time, notwithstanding that he could not trouble Phar Lap'. In the Fisher Plate there was no betting, which veteran racing writer Roy Ridgway ('Chiron' in *The Australasian*) could not recall ever having happened at Flemington. David Davis, meanwhile, was cranking up the publicity machine. From February, of course, the horse would be his, at least—the world would soon learn—on a 50/50 basis with Telford, but he left no-one in any doubt that he would now have what he had always craved . . . a say in the gelding's future program. Straight after the Cup, Davis had issued a challenge to the horse owners of the world—come to Australia and take on our champion, any distance, any amount, winner-takes-all. Within forty-eight hours, he was able to announce that the London *Daily Express* had retaliated with an invitation of their own—for Phar Lap to come to England to take on the best horses in the world at Royal Ascot. 'No,' said Davis, 'if any horse wants to race Phar Lap they will have to come to Australia to do so.' He must have known there was next to no chance of any English champion coming to Australia. Nor, given that geldings were precluded from entering most of the big-money races in England, including the Ascot Gold Cup, was there much value in Phar Lap heading for the mother country. But he had succeeded in getting into people's heads the idea of Phar Lap taking on the world.

CASHY MARTIN HAD LISTENED to Phar Lap's Melbourne Cup victory while working for his boss, Mr Munro, at the Randwick races. The wireless reception was first-class, much better than last year. Of course, by this stage Phar Lap was everyone's horse, but Cashy was still the first person who ever said he was gonna be a champion. He'd seen all of Bobby's recent wins in Sydney, and spent as much time as he could hanging round the champion's stall. He marvelled at the way Phar Lap had filled out and seemingly grown still taller, but recognised the same look in the gelding's eyes and the extraordinary bond between Bobby and Mr Woodcock. To think, Bobby was now the best horse in the world, Mr Telford was rich, Cashy's career was 'goin' all right, thanks'. Life was good.

Tuesday 25 November 1930 was Cashy Martin's seventeenth birthday. He woke early, dashed down to trackwork, and then raced back to Bowral Street for a quick bite to eat. He was in a hurry, he told his mum, because he was going to Gosford to ride his 'lucky mount', La Gloria, the filly on which he'd got his first city winner, a bit less than twelve months before. He'd also picked up the ride on an outsider called Servile in the first on the card. Hence the rush.

Gosford is a tight, turning track, situated around 70 kilometres north of Sydney. With twenty runners in the opening event the mounting yard seemed crowded, and there was a delay at the barrier as the starter tried to get the nervous field in order. Finally, they were away, and Cashy took Servile towards the lead, about four or five back, one off the fence. Approaching the three furlongs, the back-markers started to race around the pack, Cashy was suddenly caught in traffic, desperate to get out. He yanked Servile sideways, tried to get to the outside. But there was nowhere to go. A yell, 'Shit, look out!' and Servile clipped the heels in front and went down, nose first. Cashy went over the top, frozen, terrified, about to be trampled by the mob as they thundered, heavy footed, into the straight.

He was rushed to a private hospital in Gosford, in a desperately critical condition. Skull fractures, internal injuries, no chance. His mother and his elder brother, Cam, raced north, accompanied by his master's brother, the leading apprentice, Darby, and they sat by his bedside until midnight, when Cashy died. He had never regained consciousness.

'He was a great kid,' Cam Martin told a reporter the following day. 'Just starting to make headway in the racing game too. He thought of nothing else but his work.' He showed off a scrapbook Cashy had been compiling, of Phar Lap's career and his own. It started as just Phar Lap, but lately there had quite a few press clippings on the little horseman too, paragraphs on his promise, photos of various mounts. 'Geez,' his brother sobbed, flicking through the pages, 'imagine how big his book was gonna be.'

The following day, the racing fraternity rallied to the funeral. Jack Munro and several other leading Sydney trainers huddled in behind an emotional Mrs Martin, her three remaining children, Cashy's grandparents, and scores of other relatives. Seventy-five jockeys formed a guard of honour, Jim Pike among them. All his mates from Kenso primary were there. So were representatives from the AJC and the Gosford Jockey Club. Harry Telford couldn't get there in time, but was represented by Mr J. McMeekin.

Back at Braeside, little was said. Cashy had been part of the Phar Lap family. 'Thank Christ the little bloke was still here when the old boy won the Cup,' Telford growled at no-one in particular. Right at that moment, it seemed that nothing still to come would ever be the same.

CASHY MARTIN'S DEATH had a sequel on the following Saturday, when the jockeys at a meeting at Moorefield racetrack threatened to go on strike in protest over what they considered to be dangerously large fields they were obliged to ride in. Four senior riders, Ted Bartle, Maurice McCarten, Rae Johnstone and Sid Cracknell, met with stewards and though nothing was resolved the press noted that this was an unprecedented show of strength from the jockeys. The incident in race one at Gosford had clearly left them shaken. Somewhat eerily, the Truth headlined its story the next day, 'GHOST OF JOCKEY MARTIN WALKS AT MOOREFIELD'.

A change of colours

As we have seen, some regarded the decision to ban geldings from the two-year-old and three-year-old classics as a direct consequence of Phar Lap's dominance—even though the debate had been about since long before the 1929 AJC Derby. However, the VRC's next innovation—to introduce penalties and allowances in their weight-for-age races—was clearly a reaction to the Phar Lap phenomenon. The club's argument was that they had been getting a poor return for the prize money they put up; the events were poor betting races, sometimes no betting races, and many complained they were poor entertainment. After the change was announced, *The Australasian* wrote, 'The weight-for-age stakes should now be more evenly distributed, and not go to one horse.' Purists responded by saying the VRC was penalising excellence and rewarding mediocrity. Cynics claimed the decision was elitist—if it had been Carradale dominating these races, Mr Mackinnon and his mates would have been toasting his talent, not bringing him back to the field. Instead, from 1 January 1931, horses entered in the VRC's weight-for age races that had never won a weight-for-age race with a first prize of £500 or more, or a handicap with a first prize of £1000 or more, would be allowed 7 lb (three-year-olds) and 14 lb (four-year-olds and up).

Winners of a weight-for-age race worth more than £1000 would be obliged to carry a 7-lb penalty in future weight-for-age races. As well, the allowance that had been given to geldings in weight-for-age races was abolished.

Sports historians who laud the dominance of Walter Lindrum in billiards point to the 'baulk-line' rule introduced by the Billiard Association & Control Council, the sports governing body based in England, in 1932. It became known as 'Lindrum's Rule', having been devised deliberately, it seemed, to curtail the champion's propensity for remarkable high breaks. Cricket lovers remember the infamous, dangerous 'bodyline', developed again in 1932, by the English cricket captain Douglas Jardine specifically to stop Don Bradman. Most thought Jardine's tactics to be within the rules, but well outside the 'spirit' of the game. A true sign of a champion's greatness, it is argued, is when they try to change or bend the rules for the benefit of the rest of the field. In the 1930s, it was Phar Lap they tried to stop first. And to the chagrin of his legion of working-class fans, and his connections, it was not the suits from London who were behind the move, but that priggish lot from the VRC.

IN NEW SOUTH WALES, the newly elected Labor premier, Jack Lang, had introduced a 10 per cent betting tax, which lowered to rock bottom the morale of the industry in the state, already suffering following the impact of the Great Depression. Lang, never a fan of the racing clubs, whose members he saw as condescending and snobbish, was hoping the tax would bring in some much-needed government revenue. Instead it decimated the sport, especially in the country, reducing already declining attendances still further. Betting turnover and budget revenue estimates plummeted, as punters were obliged to hand over 10 per cent of the face value of their winning tickets, or take their business elsewhere. If, for example, a big punter had invested £6000 on Phar Lap in the 1930 Craven Plate, to win £1000 (thus giving him a ticket with a face value of £7000, and a tax liability of £700), he would have made only £300 profit, odds of 20–1 on, had the tax been in place. The only winners were the SP book-makers and the big operators interstate, who found themselves catering for wealthy clients calling from Sydney. By March 1931, Lang realised his mistake and limited the tax to winnings, and not the stake. This, one paper argued, should revive interest in betting in NSW, 'providing, of course, anybody has money to bet with'. It was too late, however, to save mid-week racing, which for the time being had been abandoned.

About the only big plunge the Sydney papers were able to report through January 1931 involved a moderate performer called Auda, trained by Chris O'Rourke and owned outright by David Davis, which won on 10 January after its odds firmed from double figures to 9–2. Auda wore the new Davis colours and won for her owner £3000, before tax. One unlikely feature of this race was that the mare, Queen Nassau, ran last, just as she had in Phar Lap's AJC Derby fifteen months before.

A 10 per cent impost of another kind was imposed on workers on 22 January, when the full Arbitration Court cut the basic wage by 10 per cent, arguing Australia was facing a national emergency. 'The real issue,' the judges explained, 'was whether the wage standard built up during past years of prosperity could be maintained in view of the world economic crisis and the added difficulties of local origin.' More than 30 per cent of the employable population was out of work, and in every state but Queensland the unemployment fig-ures continued to rise.

After watching Auda finish out of a place in the Challenge Stakes at Randwick on 24 January, Davis flew to Melbourne to discuss with

Telford Phar Lap's autumn campaign. Though technically the lease did not expire until February, Davis was already revelling in his new status. He'd even commissioned eminent artist Stuart Reid to paint a wonderful study of the horse, complete with Pike on top wearing the new colours, which he promptly presented to his friends at the Tattersalls Club in Sydney. A press photographer was invited to capture the handover. This before the silks had even been worn in action by Phar Lap! The meeting between Davis and Telford at Braeside was the first time the two men had ever discussed the horse's program as partners, and it was resolved that the St George Stakes at Caulfield on 14 February would see his return to the stage, followed by the Futurity Stakes, also at Caulfield. At this point, the champion was still in the VRC's main sprint, the six-furlong Newmarket Handicap, but the partners were simply waiting to see what weight he might get. When it was announced he would be asked to carry an unprecedented 11.1, an angry Telford pulled him out without even consulting Davis. 'What are they trying to do,' he complained, 'kill the horse?'

Phar Lap had never won first-up before, but so weak was the field for his return that he started at 14–1 on and scored comfortably. The Futurity Stakes the following Saturday was, however, a different matter.

Veritas: Phar Lap won the Futurity Stakes with 10.3 on his back on a single gallop after having come back from a spell at Bacchus Marsh, where he had become hog fat. Despite such a handicap, Phar Lap merely trotted and cantered and jogged until the Wednesday preceding the race. Then he opened the eyes of the Caulfield regulars by reeling off, on the sand circuit, seven furlongs in 1:30½. It sufficed!

A.B. Paterson: The Futurity Stakes at Caulfield proved that Phar Lap is still Phar Lap, which is to say that in the present writer's opinion

he is a stone ahead of any horse we have ever seen on the
Australian turf . . .

Some, Jim Pike among them, have argued that this was Phar Lap's
greatest win, or at least on par with the AJC Plate and the Melbourne
Cup. 'The good horses are set a hard task in the Caulfield Futurity,'
wrote Chiron in The Australasian. The heavy rain that soaked the course
on the Friday made matters worse, whatever Phar Lap's propensity in
the mud. He hadn't won a race over less than a mile since his solitary
victory as a two-year-old, or started in a race over less than a mile
since August 1929. Among his rivals were Mollison, the 1930
Newmarket winner, Greenline, the former AJC Sires Produce winner,
The Doctor's Orders, the South Australian speedster, Taurus, who'd
run second in an Oakleigh Plate, and Melbourne's best welter horse,
Mystic Peak. Also in the line-up was a very good galloper by the name
of Waterline, who would make a big name for himself before too
much longer. Bookmakers, as brave as they dared, bet 2–1 on.

In Pike's view, Phar Lap never went quicker, despite the weight
and the weather. This happened after he missed the start, then from
barrier one was caught on the fence, locked behind a wall of horses.
Desperate, the great rider pulled the champion back to last, and
reefed him five wide, right around the field. Meanwhile, Taurus was
highballing out in front, four lengths in front as they sped around
the corner. Phar Lap, by some estimates, was half a furlong behind
him.

The Caulfield straight is less than two furlongs, far from the
longest in Australia. Pike went to the outside, first tracking Wise
Force into the race, then dashing past him. Mollison raced to
second, with The Doctor's Orders third, but Waterline was gone,
quickly beaten by the heavy going. So, it soon became apparent, was
Mollison, whose run ended as immediately as it began. Greenline
moved to second, Phar Lap now third, but Taurus was still well clear,

though drifting out towards the middle of the track. The crowd was roaring: Phar Lap was coming hard, but was no good thing.

At the furlong, Pike changed course as Taurus crossed in front of him. Meanwhile, Mystic Peak was driving up on the inside. Half a furlong out, it seemed that any of the three could win, then Taurus' brave effort finally petered out, and Phar Lap pushed clear to defeat Mystic Peak by a pulsating neck. He was now the greatest stakes-winner in Australian racing history, moving past Amounis' previous record. Rarely, if ever, has Caulfield ever seen such a stirring struggle.

DESPITE THE NEW weight-for-age conditions, the Essendon Stakes and the King's Plate, run respectively seven and eleven days after the Futurity Stakes triumph, were both won comfortably, although the moderately performed Glare got surprisingly close in the latter race, beaten just a length and a quarter. Most critics, including the book-makers who refused to frame a straight-out market on either race, assumed Pike was kidding near the end. But he wasn't. Phar Lap was scheduled to run in the one-mile C.M. Lloyd Stakes at Flemington, just three days after the King's Plate, but suddenly that run, even his entire autumn campaign, was in jeopardy.

Jim Pike: Unfortunately, I believe that the Futurity was his undoing, at least temporarily. He wasn't then at his best, and the super-equine effort was too great a strain even for the great steel clockwork of his constitution. He was sick and sorry after the race. I warned Harry Telford to watch him carefully, because I told him it had taken a lot out of him.

Nobody realised that but me. The cheering crowd just saw his brave win. They didn't know what super effort had been necessary to win that race. Harry said he would keep a close look out, and I pointed out it would have to be a very close one. In fact, I urged him not to run again during the autumn.

Telford was all but sure the horse needed a spell, but then Phar Lap picked up, became almost chirpy. What to do? In Sydney, Davis pondered what Telford was playing at. First the horse was dreadful, then the next call said he was fine. On the Friday, however, Phar Lap was far from bright. The vet said it was kidney trouble—you'd better give him a break. Tommy Woodcock was in no doubt, and he knew the horse better than anyone. Telford wanted another opinion.

Pike was called to Caulfield, to give the horse a true test. However, before he arrived, Woodcock took the gelding for a long walk, which warmed Phar Lap up. Pike then shot him over three furlongs in 35$\frac{1}{2}$ seconds, which is impressive work at any time. 'Never better,' was the great jockey's verdict, a view he long regretted. 'Evidently he had completely deceived both of us,' Pike recalled years later, referring to himself and Telford. 'He could rise to any occasion, even when sick, and I was terribly sorry that this should have happened.'

'This' was the Lloyd Stakes. The VRC's weight-for-age penalties and allowances meant that Waterline, now on top of the ground rather than sunk in the Caulfield mud, would meet Phar Lap 21 lb better than what would have been the case under the old conditions. Despite this, but not surprisingly given that Phar Lap was shooting for a fifteenth straight victory, the books put Phar Lap up at 3–1 on, with Waterline quickly backed from 4–1 into 7–2.

Dr A.E. Syme, who had owned Braeside before Harry Telford took the lease, and his trainer Adam Skirving devised a plot to try to bring the favourite undone. Accepting with both Waterline and the 33–1 chance Temoin, they planned to send their outsider off at a rapid gallop, making Phar Lap carry every ounce of his 9.7 and leaving

Waterline to have the last crack at him. Sure enough, Temoin did go out at a furious pace, but Phar Lap, listless at the barrier, jumped poorly, and found himself two lengths *behind* Waterline and eight lengths adrift of the pacemaker. It was all Pike could do to keep in touch. Previously, even in the Futurity, Pike had been content to ride the great horse quietly, knowing he was either winning easily or doing his best. Now, though, he pushed the gelding as hard and per-sistently as he had ever driven a horse in his life. Coming to the turn, the champion seemed to lift, and at the two furlongs the three horses were level. Temoin, exhausted, dropped back, as Phar Lap sneaked a neck clear, to the roars of the crowd. But then Billy Duncan on Waterline got busy and by the finish was a neck in front and edging away. 'He [Phar Lap] seemed to climb a bit near home,' Chiron wrote in *The Australasian*, 'and some people thought he did the same when he beat Glare in the King's Plate.'

Straight after the race, Telford approached Sol Green and asked if he could take Phar Lap up to Bacchus Marsh. Once there, he hoped the horse would recover in time to make the trip to the Sydney autumn carnival, but within days it was obvious that a long spell was called for. The 'kidney trouble' had returned, worse than ever. David Davis would not be able to show off his horse to his Sydney associ-ates until the spring. Initially, he had been desperate to conquer Sydney once again, but when he saw for himself how much his horse was struggling, he quickly concurred that a spell was necessary. He had, in fact, harboured his own worries about the gelding since before the Futurity, when he went out to Caulfield to see his charge and was shown the horse's badly cracked heels. Telford hadn't been kidding—the horse was not as flash as they needed him to be. How Phar Lap won the Futurity two days later, Davis had no idea.

SO SYDNEY WAS OUT, but Davis had much grander plans. Continuing the theme he had first expounded to the press immediately after the 1930 Melbourne Cup, he admitted off the record that he was keen to take his horse to the United States and had welcomed overtures from the Agua Caliente Race Club, which was run by Americans but based in Tijuana, just beyond the US/Mexico border. In *The Arrow*, J.F. Dexter wrote, 'We continue to read that Phar Lap will yet go to America or England, but I would like to bet against it . . .'

Davis, however, was already on his way to America to talk business. He sought guarantees involving the weight his horse would receive, the covering of expenses, and introductions to other race clubs across the country. The Agua Caliente Club, led by their president, James Crofton, were totally accommodating. They saw in the Australian champion an international angle that might set their event apart from the big races run later in the year on the other side of the country. Davis compared their gestures and enthusiasm to the barriers the Australian racing clubs were putting in the way of his horse. He, like Telford, blamed the VRC's weight-for-age penalties and allowances for the end of Phar Lap's winning streak as much as he blamed the horse's illness. By the time he was ready to return to Australia in late May, he and Crofton had shaken on a deal. Harry Telford would find out soon enough.

Davis was thinking big at a time when some Australian racing clubs were going to the wall. The Depression was biting hard, especially so in South Australia and Queensland, and in country NSW and Victoria. Stakes were being reduced all over the country, as was betting turnover, and the VRC announced that the Melbourne Cup for 1931 would be worth $7200, the smallest prize since Prince Foote's Cup in 1909. The booming days immediately before the financial crash of the 1890s—Carbine's Cup had been worth as much as Phar

Lap's forty years later—now truly seemed a lifetime ago, never to be repeated.

Examples of the ravenous times were everywhere. The Queensland Turf Club announced it was cutting prize money across the board by one-third. The Albury Race Club, once one of the strongest in the bush, cut the stakes for its Gold Cup race from £1000 to £400. The accountants at the Orange Jockey Club, in western New South Wales, revealed that revenue from a two-day meeting in early 1931 amounted to a fraction less than £137, as against £1269 for the same days in 1930. These financial plights, while grave for the clubs involved and the racing industry as a whole, paled beside the social dislocation and personal heartbreak that went with the loss of jobs, food on the table and hope. One of the myths of these times is that the masses constantly put what pennies they had on Phar Lap, as if the great horse alone could fight off the worst of the bad times. There was, no doubt, a cynical feeling in some sections of the community that Phar Lap was a safer investment than the banks, but the odds about him were too prohibitive and the money to bet with was just not there. More than once, punters who did back him on the on-course totalisator actually lost money, because the percentage taken out of the pool by tax and the clubs was greater than that put on the rest of the field. But like Bradman scoring hundreds, and unlike just about every horse before or since, Phar Lap kept winning, race after race. In these fickle and for many hopeless times, that surety was greatly valued. At various times, both Sydney and Melbourne laid claim to him; he was the horse of the people.

Splits in the stable

Phar Lap's Melbourne Cup weight for 1931, announced in late June, was 10.10, one pound less than he received for the Caulfield Cup. Most thought it fair, even though it was 5 lb more than Carbine was allotted in 1890, his five-year-old year. Only Archer, who was given 11.4 after winning the first two Cups in 1861 and 1862, the great horse of the 1860s, The Barb, 11.7 in 1869, and Carbine, 10.12 in 1891, had ever received more. No horse had ever started with such an impost. Telford remarked that a Cup start was definitely a possibility, as the champion had recovered well. Tommy Woodcock revealed in 1936 that rather than simply let his great mate enjoy the good life at Underbank, he also gave him a series of long canters on Sol Green's main paddock, plus plenty of regular walks across the property. So glowing were his reports to Telford, he was able to convince the trainer to leave him at Bacchus Marsh for much longer than was originally intended.

Tommy Woodcock: It was while on that vacation at Underbank I learned a horse could be conditioned without pumping fast work and plenty of it into him ... I had Phar Lap in great trim [but] he was brought to Melbourne to all intents and purposes a horse just in from a five-month spell.

Track watchers, trainers and the general race-going army naturally thought a six- or eight-week preparation would be required to get him fighting fit. I knew he was good enough to beat the Underwood Stakes opposition to a frazzle. But Harry Telford had Rondalina entered for the race, and he did not think Phar Lap was sufficiently advanced to give that filly 22lb. She had won the Chatswood Plate at Caulfield earlier in the month and Harry was wrapped up in her ...

Pike had journeyed south for the champ's comeback to racing, in the Underwood Stakes at Williamstown, but the weather intervened and the meeting was put off to the following Tuesday, which left the great horseman in a quandary. He needed to be back in Sydney as soon as possible. Telford doubted Phar Lap was ready to win, but Woodcock had told him Phar Lap was a good thing.

'Tommy,' he said, 'he'd have to be a marvel to win the Underwood.'

'But he is a marvel, Jim,' Woodcock replied.

'Sure, Tommy, he's a daddy all right, and I'm sorry I've made arrangements to go.'

Tommy Woodcock: Heavy rain had the track at Braeside in such a state that it was impossible to gallop Phar Lap and I knew that he wanted only one rousing gallop to make him a good thing for the Underwood. I rang Stan Boyden, Chapman's float driver, and asked him to get in touch with Mr A.V. Hiskens, secretary of the Moonee Valley Racing Club, and arrange if possible to give some horses a gallop on the Monday afternoon on his track. Mr Hiskens consented.

In the gallop at the Valley, Phar Lap more than pleased me by running a mile in 1:45$^{1}/_{2}$, and I felt certain that my plans had been timed to the day.

Tuesday was universally recognised as being the worst racing day of the week, but fortunately for the Williamstown Club they had two star attractions—the new totalisator (making its second appearance in Melbourne, having had its debut at Moonee Valley the previous week) and, of course, Phar Lap. 'He looks as big as a cart-horse!' one keen observer chortled when the gelding's rug was finally removed in the mounting yard, and Phar Lap went out at 2–1, with Wise Force and Waterline next in commission and Rondalina at 33s. The result was a stable quinella, in the order Woodcock, but not Telford, would have predicted. 'It will be a long time,' Chiron wrote afterwards, 'before anybody will get another chance of backing him at anything like those odds in a weight-for-age race. Phar Lap has built up and furnished right up to his great frame, and he is now a really magnificent horse in every way.'

Phar Lap and Rondalina ran 1–2 again eleven days later in the Memsie Stakes at Caulfield, after which they headed to Sydney. Davis, meanwhile, was in constant communication with James Crofton, and with all the details dotted and crossed, information was released to the Californian press that 'Australia's wonder horse, Phar Lap' would be coming to North America around 1 January to prepare for the Agua Caliente Handicap. 'An agreement,' the reports continued, 'is being drawn up between [David] Davis and the Agua Caliente JC assuring his [Phar Lap's] invasion of the American turf.' The release also suggested that Phar Lap might be racing at Arlington, Hawthorne and Belmont Park as well and that Pike was scheduled to travel with the horse to ride him in his American engagements.

This last point, that Pike would cross the Pacific to be the jockey, could not have been true. Whether David Davis would have realised this is unknown, but those closest to Pike were aware that he deplored sea travel. As a lad he'd sailed to England with his master,

Bill Kelso. The pair returned to Australia after a relatively short stay, but Pike wanted to go back and set sail again for England. However, this second journey was so awful and dangerous that when the ship docked in Colombo the young jockey stopped, gritted his teeth and came straight back, vowing never to set foot on a ship again once he got back to dry Australia. In all the years after, he never sailed to Melbourne for a big meeting, as his wife sometimes did. He preferred to drive or take the train.

When Davis arrived back in Australia in time for the AJC's spring carnival, he dismissed the US reports as mere speculation. Yes, he would like to race Phar Lap in America. But his co-owner did not. No, nothing has been confirmed. I assure you, there is nothing more to say. Good morning, gentlemen. The pressmen were left to wonder; the report seemed so sure. For the next five weeks Davis refused to confirm but often denied the basis of the story. About the only certainty surrounding Phar Lap was that he just kept on winning.

Musket: Phar Lap makes records only for the purpose of breaking them, and he made another in the Craven Plate on Wednesday by reducing the time to 2:2^1/$_2$. After the race people were speculating about how much he could have reduced that time had he been really extended, as at no part of the race was he at his top. The Epsom Handicap favourite, Pentheus, set out to break him up if possible, and in the first furlong or so drew out with a five-lengths lead. Phar Lap reduced it to two without the least effort, and after that Pike allowed him to trail the leader until they reached the straight. Then he gave Phar Lap his head. Pentheus was gathered up in a few strides and then Phar Lap strode home at his leisure.

Phar Lap's return for his three weeks in Sydney was four wins from four starts. Bookies never framed a straight-out market on any of the races. Editors were clamouring for stories about the great champion, but the races themselves offered little. In the Hill Stakes at Rosehill, Phar Lap's three rivals, including the Doncaster Handicap winner Sir Chrystopher, let the favourite go off on his own and fought each other for second place. Only one opponent, the well-performed New Zealander Chide, turned up for the Randwick Plate. In desperation, the racing writers stepped back twelve months and tried to pester Telford and Davis into revealing their Cup plans, and Davis and Telford stepped back with them and refused to reveal a thing. Doubles betting as a consequence was paralysed. So weak is the Caulfield Cup field, one report hypothesised, they'll definitely run. What, and risk a 10-lb penalty, another countered. Telford reckons the weight's too much, he'll keep him for the weight-for-age events. But he can't: Davis promised the Americans he'd win the Melbourne Cup.

Davis, it was rumoured, had strongly supported a Cups double that began with the lightweight hope, Royal Barb, and finished with Phar Lap. 'It is known beyond doubt,' countered Banjo Paterson, 'that the Phar Lap stable secured a big double about Vigne [an impressive recent winner of the Rosehill Cup] and Phar Lap.' In early October, at the Tattersalls Club in Sydney, Davis announced Phar Lap would definitely start at Flemington, unless a top lightweight or out-standing three-year-old emerged. What about Caulfield? 'I think intending doubles backers should stay their hand,' advised Davis, which frustrated the punters and pundits no end. The punters wanted to punt.

For Harry Telford, owning the best racehorse since Carbine had become just about too much to bear. He was resisting Davis' American dream, but the damn man's persistence was wearing him down. After all the horse has done for us, why put him through a stressful voyage across the Pacific? Finally, they agreed to take him out of the Caulfield Cup, but not until after Telford had confessed to a journalist that he'd 'given Phar Lap up' because racing the horse was 'killing' the trainer. When he saw the quote in print he back-tracked, saying he'd been misinterpreted, but he did admit that Davis now had the major say in what the horse would do, a precursor to future developments concerning the Melbourne Cup and beyond.

Telford was also becoming increasingly exasperated with Woodcock's ever-growing belief that he, Woodcock, knew more about training Phar Lap than Telford did. Telford had basically handed over the care of the gelding to Woodcock during the winter break at Underbank, to the point of leaving him up there for longer than he would have liked because the strapper suggested it would help, rather than hinder, the spring campaign. He recognised that Woodcock had the makings of a master horseman, to the point of recommending to his owners when the idea of opening a Sydney arm of the Telford training operation was mooted that Woodcock was the man to run that venture. This concept reached the point where Woodcock applied for and got his No. 1 trainer's licence in Sydney, but the concept never materialised, perhaps because Woodcock eventually decided that he preferred to stay with Phar Lap.

It was Woodcock's hard-held opinion that the champion didn't need a lot of tough training to get him to his peak, whereas Telford was a firm believer in work and then some. The first-up win at Williamstown, despite the fact he looked well out of condition, and the astonishing performance in the Craven Plate in Sydney suggest Woodcock might have been right, but Telford still bristled when told by someone half his age and with a skerrick of his experience and know-how that he didn't know what was best for the horse. Still, he stayed up at Braeside with the majority of his team and left Woodcock at Caulfield to follow orders and supervise his superstar's Cup preparation.

For two weeks after his return from Sydney, Phar Lap's work at Caulfield had consisted of no more than a few trots on the sand track, interspersed by an occasional canter. Observers were totally baffled by this strategy. It hardly seemed the way to get a horse ready to carry 10.10 in a two-mile race. But then the horse came out and comfortably won the Cox Plate, beating two classy three-year-olds, Chatham and Johnnie Jason. The season's best three-year-old to that point, the gelding Ammon Ra, had been scratched from the race because his trainer could see no value in taking on Phar Lap. A brilliant New Zealander, Ammon Ra, after spectacular wins in the AJC Derby and the Caulfield Guineas, was being spoken of in all parts as the next big thing.

Tommy Woodcock: I suppose I was a bit foolish, and should have gave him more work than what I did ... So anyhow, the Cox Plate come up and 'course Phar Lap won it quite easy. And, 'course, not having had much work he did blow a little bit, and he pulled up a bit big, and I decided, you know, that he was a bit big. And, of course, Harry come up to me and he said, 'There yer go—I told you—look at him! He's too fat—miles too fat,' he said. 'I want about three months to get him ready for the Melbourne Cup.' And away he went ... Oh, it nearly used to make me cry, truly, the way he worked him. He just galloped the inside out of him all the week.

Telford wanted to take Phar Lap out of the Cup. However, Davis had his heart set on the trophy, and Telford knew that given what had happened in the past no-one, least of all the VRC committee, would believe him if he said he was acting in the best interests of the horse by scratching him. They'd assume there was some sinister plot behind the move. So, from first light Monday, the angry trainer took charge, stunning the same track touts who'd previously been baffled by the horse's lack of hard work. Phar Lap was galloped on five mornings straight over varying distances, from seven furlongs to a mile and a quarter, always on the sand track. 'You would search in vain,' wrote one veteran racing scribe later, 'for another horse who would stand up to such galloping.'

TELFORD HAS BEEN PAINTED in years since as a trainer who worked his horses, and specifically Phar Lap, astonishingly hard. There is no doubt that he appreciated the value of hard work and liked his horses tough, but there is much evidence, in trackwork times and press reports, to suggest that, at least often in the champion's career, he relied on long, slow work to bring his star to his peak. Barring his final bit of work before a big race, Phar Lap was usually a fair way from recording the best time of the morning. Never was the horse rushed early in a preparation. However, on this occasion it is clear that an overwrought Telford over-reacted. By the Saturday of the Melbourne Stakes Phar Lap was all but flattened. Before the race, Woodcock told Jim Pike that the champ was no good thing but Pike, aware of the feud between Telford and Woodcock, dismissed this as a case of the strapper trying to get one-up on his boss. Afterwards, though, the jockey was most concerned.

> **Jim Pike:** He had the race well won two furlongs from home, and right until within 50 yards of the post was travelling well, but suddenly I felt him falter, and I badly wanted to shift that winning post back towards me. But fortunately I held him together, and the others didn't realise my plight. So he got there. But only by a half a length, mark you, and I wonder how many realised he was flat out to do that!
>
> I told Harry Telford what had happened and suggested scratching

him and turning him out. But that stirred up a hornet's nest. Who was going to scratch a 6–4 favourite from a Melbourne Cup?

Telford wanted out. Woodcock wanted out. Pike wanted out. After the Melbourne Stakes, Telford and Davis got embroiled in a vigorous discussion over the race on Tuesday. Finally, it came down to who would go to the VRC offices to scratch the horse. 'If he runs on Tuesday,' argued Telford, 'you might ruin him. Then what will you be taking to America?' So Davis headed up to see Lachlan Mackinnon.

Late on Saturday night, racing writer Bert Wolfe tracked down Davis at the Alexander Hotel in Melbourne. Immediately, Wolfe asked the question on the lips of the nation.

'Mr Davis, are you going to be running Phar Lap?'

Davis looked up slowly. 'I have no choice,' he replied. 'The VRC says I must.'

Mackinnon had told him, as legend has it, that he'd be scratching the horse at his own peril. The VRC chairman, suddenly a champion for the masses, said he believed those who'd wagered on Phar Lap in pre-post markets deserved a run for their money.

BACK ON AJC DERBY DAY 1929, when L.K.S. Mackinnon and his associates from the Australian Jockey Club, were chatting in the members' bar at Randwick, the nation's economic future was looking awfully grim. A little more than two years later, as they sipped on their whiskies at Flemington early on Victoria Derby Day 1931, things were looking a good deal brighter. Most agreed that they'd seen the worst of it, and toasted the fact that none of the major breeders had gone to the wall. There were definitely more visitors from interstate. The chairman of the South Australian Jockey Club was there, hinting that racing in Adelaide was faring much better, thank you, than it had been just a few months before. A colleague from Perth said much the same thing. They gazed over towards the Paddock, stopping for a moment to study the Flat.

'This is as good an attendance for Derby Day as we've had for what, five years?' asked Mr Kewney, the VRC Secretary, who'd been appointed to the position in 1925.

'Perhaps not that long,' Mr Mackinnon countered, 'but I'd say we're back now to where we were about a decade back, before the post-war boom.'

Committeemen spoke positively about the news from Canberra, where it seemed that the Scullin Labor government was doomed. The split in the Labor ranks, precipitated by forces loyal to the New South Wales Premier, Jack Lang, seemed bent on destroying federal Labor and there was even talk of an election prior to Christmas. Given all the hardship over the past two years, and the apparent inability of Scullin and his Cabinet to do anything about it, a fresh vote would almost certainly mean the conservatives, led by Joseph Lyons, would regain office.

Still the machinations of federal parliament meant much less to the person on the street than did the latest gossip on the VRC carnival. The sensation of the first day had been the defeat of Ammon Ra in the Derby. At 7–2 on, the third shortest favourite in the history of the race (after Phar Lap, at 9–2 on in 1929, and Poseidon, 4–1 on in 1906), he finished fourth, behind Johnnie Jason, Chatham and Voil d'Amour. Johnnie Jason won, Chiron wrote, 'not because of his superiority over his eight rivals, but because of the genius of Pike'. Of the controversy surrounding Pike's mount in the Cup, The Australasian's racing man was less effusive.

Chiron: People are becoming bored with the air of mystery and sensation that surrounds Phar Lap. His owners have been weary of it for more than a year and would welcome relief from the fierce light of publicity thrown upon them. Their lives have been made a burden by insistent demands during the last few weeks that they should declare their intentions regarding the horse in connection with the Melbourne Cup. They made a declaration over a month ago, when Mr Davis said it was intended to start Phar Lap in the Melbourne Cup unless the conditions on the day were unfavourable or in the meantime some horse of exceptional merit with a light weight in the Cup or an outstanding three-year-old came to light. There did not seem to be any more to be said on the subject, but day after day both Mr Davis and Telford were hunted down and asked to say whether Phar Lap would start in the Cup or not. Ownership of a public racing idol has its drawbacks as well as its advantages.

After the attempt to shoot him on Derby Day last year, when he was returning from the Caulfield tracks, Phar Lap spent the weekend under guard at St Albans, near Geelong and on Cup Day was escorted from St Albans to Flemington by police guard. Apparently there was a fear that something similar might happen again this year, and on Saturday morning four plain-clothes police were detailed to watch Phar Lap until he completed his engagement in the Melbourne Cup. Why anybody should want to do him an injury is difficult to imagine because there was no reason for it. Last year, large sums of money were laid against him by the bookmakers, but that was not the case this year, as there was no market for him in either of the Cups in Melbourne or Sydney. When a favourite is to be 'nobbled' there must be a motive, but where was the motive this year?

Nearly all the bets against Phar Lap have been laid by the leading members of the ring, and they are not the type of men likely to descend to foul or unfair methods to prevent him winning.

At present, the racing world appears to be suffering from Phar Lap hysteria ...

As on Derby Day, the crowd for the Cup far exceeded expectations, with upwards of 90,000 paying to get into Flemington. Fourteen thousand pounds would be bet through the new totalisator on the Cup alone.

Phar Lap had been 6–4 on Saturday, now early takers on Cup Day were offered 2–1, but the rumours about his condition were all negative. By start time, he was still favourite, but 3–1, the best odds bet about him since September 1929. Astonishingly, Telford had given his charge another rousing gallop over a mile on the Monday morning, which reduced his relationship with Woodcock to its lowest ebb. In the mounting yard, he was of course the centre of attention, and some observers remarked how good Phar Lap looked. But Pike and Woodcock, and Telford too, knew better.

After Telford legged Pike up, Woodcock walked him around the ring as he'd done so many times before. Only this time he did so with a heavy, apprehensive heart.

'Don't worry, son,' Pike whispered to him, 'when he's had enough, I won't knock him around.'

Veritas: The race knocked him out. That was the reason for his subsequent non-appearance at the meeting . . . Many there are who, to this day, think that Phar Lap might have done better in the Cup. Had they intently watched Pike ride him to the last gasp, they would realise that in all probability the jockey's trying endeavours, coupled with the 150 lb he carried, reduced Phar Lap to a similar condition of health as after the C.M. Lloyd Stakes.

The race, for the third year in a row, was desperately slow, which allowed White Nose, all but ignored until his win in the Hotham Handicap on Derby Day, to lead just about all the way. Phar Lap, from the outside barrier, was sixth when they went past the winning post on the first lap, and held his position, though out three wide, until the six furlongs. Then Pike stirred the favourite, and he edged forward. 'Here he comes!' cheered his supporters on the Flat, but the move was short-lived and it was apparent before the corner that Carbine's weight-carrying record was not in jeopardy. At the furlong, Concentrate, the horse who'd run Phar Lap to a half-length in the Melbourne Stakes, made a dash, but just as it seemed he might run White Nose down, his sprint ended abruptly and he dropped back, to hang onto third. Shadow King ran past him into second place. Phar Lap, meanwhile, was running at his own speed into eighth place. Later it was confirmed that Concentrate had broken down.

EVEN THOUGH HE was crying out for a break, Phar Lap was an acceptor in the C.B. Fisher Plate, to be run, as usual, on the Saturday after the Cup. On the Friday Davis was asked if his horse would run. 'Yes he will,' Davis replied.

On the Saturday morning, he went out to Braeside. 'What do you think?' he asked Telford. 'It's a weak field. There's easy money to be made.' Telford could stand no more. He spun around, but before he could say anything, Woodcock cried, 'Start him and you risk ruining him for good!' Without a word, Telford walked to the phone, called the scratchings office at Flemington, and took the champion out, leaving Davis to face the wrath of the VRC committeemen at the course later in the day. Pathetically, the American told reporters the horse had needed some dental work which he had not been aware of. The Fisher Plate was ruined, reduced to just two starters. By the time Veilmond and Idle Banter jumped away in what had become their match race, Woodcock and Phar Lap were on a horse float, bound for a few days' rehabilitation at Bacchus Marsh.

DAVID DAVIS FINALLY CONFIRMED racing's worst kept rumour on the Monday, when he announced breathlessly that Phar Lap was going to the United States to compete in the Agua Caliente Handicap. Most journalists rolled with the punchline. The report published back in late September had been right in every respect, bar the incorrect assertion that Pike would be the jockey. Arrangements had been made to transport the horse to New Zealand, leaving Sydney on Friday 20 November, on the good ship *Ulimaroa*, the plan being to let the horse rest up there for a few weeks before setting sail for San Francisco. Telford would not be going, purportedly because he felt obliged to the rest of his horses, although there were strong whispers about that he was far from happy with the whole concept of Phar Lap going offshore. The trainer's responsibility had been given to Woodcock. Pike's job went to Billy Elliott.

Davis, to his credit, had garnered a considerable bargain from the Agua Caliente Club. All expenses were covered. Consequently, Telford was able to go to outrageous lengths to prepare Phar Lap's quarters for the voyage from New Zealand to California in a way that would give the horse as comfortable a journey as possible. On the deck of the vessel, *Monowai*, would be three special enclosures, all covered with coir matting and one topped with sand; whenever the gelding wanted a sand roll, he could have one. The three pieces of matting required measured around 8 x 6 metres, 6 x 3.5 metres, and 4.5 x 1.2 metres. Phar Lap's box was padded, well lit and well ventilated.

First, though, the champion had to get to New Zealand, in onboard conditions not dissimilar to those he'd endured during his voyage in the opposite direction nearly four years before. Telford was at the dock in Sydney, along with a big crowd, to farewell the great horse and Woodcock. Though the mood appeared cheery as the *Ulimaroa* set off, once they were clear of the Harbour the ocean turned angry, giving Phar Lap and his new trainer a difficult time. Woodcock recalled later that the horse handled the big swell better than he did, but once in the land of Phar Lap's birth they both settled in nicely at Hugh Telford's property at Trentham, where Harry Telford had arranged for the horse to be stabled. The plan was for the champion to stay there for the best part of six weeks, perhaps longer if Davis could not get rock-solid commitments from the Americans. But provided everything was in order, they would continue on to the US, leaving New Zealand in the last week of 1931.

Apprentice Jack Martin and veterinary surgeon Bill Nielsen left for New Zealand on the *Monowai*—complete with Harry Telford's custom-built equine equivalent of first class—not long before Christmas, meeting up with Woodcock and the champion in Wellington. Then it was all aboard for San Francisco.

David Davis: I feel fully justified in taking Phar Lap from Australia. Since the horse has defeated everything there, there was nothing left for me to do but take him to America.

His visit to America is a gamble with the climate, water and other conditions, but Phar Lap is wonderfully good tempered and easily adapts himself to conditions. I have been away too long to know just what American racing conditions are, but if I get as square a deal here as I got in Australia I will be well pleased.

While Davis was justifying his move in the American press, *The Referee*'s Victorian correspondent was writing, 'H. Telford has become quite a convivial soul since he has been rid of Phar Lap, the worry of whom, he asserts, had him on the verge of dementia. He has leased a few of his horses to fellow trainers and all going well, Phar Lap's discoverer may visit New Zealand for the yearling sales in the New Year.'

At Trentham, Phar Lap became a huge attraction, drawing a crowd day after day. New Zealanders had never stopped reminding Australians that Phar Lap was actually a Kiwi by birth, and never would. Although Woodcock restricted the times when the horse was on show, he was the perfect host, allowing young children to be photographed atop the great champion, and selling imprints of his hoof to the public, with proceeds going to a local charity. And with Hugh Telford's help, and following Harry Telford's instructions, he stockpiled as much high-quality New Zealand feed as he could muster, for the journey to California and the stay at Agua Caliente.

Courtesy of the Agua Caliente Club and its chairman, James Crofton, barely a day went by without a press release exhorting the deeds and ability of the 'Red Terror', many of which amused and astonished the turf writers back in Australia. But despite the PR campaign, things were not looking too bright in Mexico and it was grimly announced just after Christmas that the club had lost upwards of $100,000 so far in December. Meetings had been scheduled for six days a week right through to the climax—the $100,000 Handicap—on 20 March, but a temporary halt was called and rumours abounded that the stake for the big race was to be reduced. Davis met Crofton in San Diego, to be told racing would resume on New Year's Day, and immediately cabled Woodcock in Wellington to get the horse on board. Within a matter of hours, he learned that the *Monowai* had left for the Cook Islands; not long after the Agua Caliente Club announced that sadly, because of cost cutting, it had no alternative but to cut the stake in their feature race to $50,000.

Bill Stutt (President of Moonee Valley Race Club for twenty-five years): They gave Tom a very nice cabin on this boat, he was very happy. And the first night out he was down having his dinner in the dining area when one of the crew came rushing in, saying, 'Quick,

your horse has gone berserk!' Phar Lap was up on deck in a big box.
So Tom rushed up and as soon as he got there Phar Lap quietened
down—it was just that Tom wasn't with him. So the lovely cabin Tom
got was useless because for the whole trip to America he slept in the
horse's box with the horse.

I remember saying to him once—he occasionally would sleep
with the horse in Melbourne, in the box with him, particularly before
a big race—'Tom, wouldn't you be worried that he might roll on
you?'

'Oh no, Bill, he wouldn't roll on me. Oh, no.'

It never occurred to him that there was any risk. So the whole way
to America he slept in the box with the horse!

Phar Lap arrived in San Francisco on 15 January, to be greeted by a
snowstorm. Davis and a number of representatives from Agua
Caliente, Californian racing and the media were there to greet the
party. When Davis theatrically asked if Phar Lap's rugs could be
removed, to prove to the waiting journalists just what a powerful
specimen his Aussie champion was, Woodcock, tired and apprehensive, refused as politely as he could.

One man who saw Phar Lap disembark was an Australian dentist,
Frank Campbell, who at the time had a practice at nearby Oakland.
Later he saw the champion of whom he had heard so much, both
from friends back home and via the constant stream of publicity
blurbs in the local press, and commented, 'Woodcock has Phar Lap
in wonderful condition. He looks a cut above the American cracks,
has a much more commanding appearance and a great stride. He'll
win the Agua Caliente Handicap with three or four lengths to spare.'

One of the greatest achievements of Woodcock and his team was
to sustain Phar Lap throughout the long and inevitably arduous
voyage. Telford's meticulous efforts in getting the champion's

quarters right—which he could do because of Davis' shrewd bargaining that had the Agua Caliente club covering any and all expenses—were clearly clever and effective. Through January, though, Davis would have an awful time getting the Americans to confirm all details of their Mexican adventure.

J.F. Dexter: Mr Davis, part owner of Phar Lap, complains that the vacillating attitude of the proprietors concerning whether or not the Agua Caliente will be on for his champion gives him a daily headache. A touch of the sauce he fed to the public, books and the press when Phar Lap was or wasn't going to run in the last Melbourne Cup, eh?

It's a long way to Caliente

By 27 January, finally, Phar Lap was in Agua Caliente, reportedly showing no ill-effects from the 965-kilometre drive down the Californian coast. Australian sports papers had been running regular updates and comments from the US, although in most cases these were simply cabled press releases that were either reproduced naively or ridiculed for their exaggerations. The following year, when asked about Phar Lap, the veteran American racing writer C.E. Brossman would comment, 'Probably no horse was better advertised than was Phar Lap when he first arrived in this country. Special writers were detailed to ballyhoo the horse from the time he was placed on board ship.'

In reality, however, little was known of what or how the horse was doing. Phar Lap's first public appearance in Mexico was to be on 7 February; until then Woodcock wanted the horse to be 'thoroughly familiar with his surroundings'. The curious and suspicious were being kept from Phar Lap's stable by armed guards. According to one source, an exhibition race two or three weeks before the big Handicap had been programmed, for which Davis would be hand-somely paid. The horse had been worked over two miles, with Martin up. No, another paragraph countered, he hadn't been worked at all. Adding a new angle, Jack Farrell, a former Sydney City alderman who had just returned from a world tour, recalled his visit to Agua Caliente. 'It is a sanatorium for jaded and overworked American thieves and gangsters,' he said. 'Just before I left, they stole the gold plate out of the mouth of a sleeping citizen. If Woodcock isn't careful, he'll wake up one morning and find Phar Lap gone.'

The Hipodromo del Agua Caliente was a hotel resort, casino, golf course and racetrack complex located on the outskirts of Tijuana. It had been conceived in the 1920s as a reaction to Prohibition in the US, and offered Americans, predominantly rich Californians, a chance to slip over the border and enjoy their punting and drinking legally in lavish surroundings. America's biggest stars often came south to entertain patrons. From November 1931 to the last week of March 1932 (save for that postponement in late December), racing was conducted six days a week, Tuesday to Sunday, rich gamblers leaving their places at the roulette tables to watch the action from a plush grandstand that seated 5000 people.

Those punters would have been disappointed and mystified when Phar Lap's exhibition race was cancelled without explanation. And they would have been confused in early March when word came that Phar Lap was in trouble. He had stepped on a stone during work on the pebbly tracks and damaged a hoof. Woodcock later blamed the injury on the shoes Telford had told him to use on the horse. He should have listened to the local experts, he reckoned. But how serious was the setback?

The Australasian: There always has been an air of mystery about Phar Lap, and the policy adopted in Australia with him is apparently being pursued in Mexico, as according to the cable messages he is being kept 'under lock and key and nobody is allowed to enter the stable'.

Martin, one of Phar Lap's attendants, declared that the horse will be all right again in a few days. Martin was evidently right, as Phar Lap has worked since.

There was a suspicion that the hoof injury was a ruse, to get his supporters better odds. In fact, Woodcock feared revealing the seriousness of the injury, given that Phar Lap was such a drawcard for the main event. He gave great credit to a Canadian farrier, Jimmy Smith, and to Bill Nielsen for getting the horse right in time.

Before, during and after this affair, track watchers were astounded by the Australians' training methods, which eschewed the American method of plenty of short, fast work. Phar Lap had not been through even one public speed test, instead his public work had been restricted to walking and jogging. Woodcock would get no more than enough to cover his expenses if the horse was beaten, but was bravely backing his own beliefs. 'I do not know why they should be criticising our training methods,' he said to an Australian press representative. 'We brought Phar Lap up to several of his victories in just the same way. We do not believe in permitting a horse to run his race in a workout. We want him to give everything he has on Sunday.'

Daily Racing Form (a US publication): Clockers believe that Phar Lap may have done some secret work on the small training track which is half a mile distant from the main track. Many horses train there at odd hours, away from the prying eyes. There is also a ring in a level dell of a canyon about 400 yards directly south of Phar Lap's stable door. Well-beaten paths lead in its direction. In this dell, trainer Woodcock obtains the green grass for Phar Lap's daily fare and it is known that Phar Lap has visited there. A suspicion exists in clockers' minds that Phar Lap may have been a busy horse all the time he was supposed to be laid up.

Part of Woodcock's brief was to keep details of the gelding's work secret, so his boss could get the most lucrative odds possible. Later he would explain how he had deceived the locals. Apparently, a track tout had been posted in the grandstand all night, to make sure he saw any fast work by the Aussie invader if it happened pre-dawn, and only departed after Phar Lap had again done no more than canter slowly around the track. However, on three occasions after this charade had been played out and the tout had left for breakfast, Woodcock had Jack Martin or Billy Elliott bring Phar Lap back to gallop in good time. In on the scam was Bert Wolfe, the Australian journalist who had travelled to Mexico to cover the drama for a number of papers back home. The scheme worked brilliantly. Davis later told friends the average price he got about his champion was 4–1, to win $50,000. Not all this, though, was his—his Sydney trainer, Chris O'Rourke, was one who revealed later that Davis had got top odds for him as well. By post time, Phar Lap was 6–5.

In the seven days leading up to the Handicap, the publicity campaign moved into top gear. One press release had Woodcock grandly saying, 'We will do what Epinard and Papyrus failed to do when they invaded America. This Phar Lap is a greater horse than either the French or the English racer, and that will be shown on Sunday.' Elliott, in similar bold tones, raved, 'Nothing will beat Phar Lap. I know the horse and what he can do. Phar Lap will win by half a furlong.' At the official pre-race press conference, Mr Crofton, Chairman of the Club, described his star attraction as 'One of the most beautiful specimens of a thoroughbred I have ever laid my eyes on.'

Snowy Baker: Phar Lap's presence is creating a great stir. In times gone by, Australia held the world's best boxers, tennis players, swimmers and others, but in recent years other lands and the USA have won the blue ribands with their athletes. Let us hope the wonder horse will beat the best and our young Australian men and women will start to retrieve what were once ours.

Reginald 'Snowy' Baker remains arguably Australia's greatest ever all-round sportsman. He represented his country in a variety of sports, including boxing, rugby and polo, and was also an outstanding swimmer and water polo player. Later, he was a high-profile sports promoter and occasional journalist, before moving to California where he hoped to make it in the movies but instead found himself acting as a stuntman and being polo and riding teacher to the stars. At the 1908 Olympics, he'd won a silver medal as a middleweight boxer, beaten by an Englishman in a bout refereed and judged by the Pom's father. He knew how hard it was to make it on the world stage. He couldn't conquer America; could Phar Lap?

At Braeside, Harry Telford was on the phone, chatting to his old comrade Bob Price. 'Woodcock's cabled,' Telford told his friend, 'to say the horse's a certainty. He reckons Phar Lap's never been better, and that I should have a good bet.' Woodcock would recall sending that cable. 'In code, I asked him how much he wanted invested,' he said. 'No reply came. Thus Phar Lap was running for half the stake only for Telford.'

Up in Sydney, the Vacuum Oil Company announced that the big race would be broadcast live across the country, on 2UW, 3DB, 4BC, 5AD and 6ML, from 8 a.m. on Monday morning. Plus, the company would sponsor a special preview of the event on Saturday evening. These were heady times. Not only was the economy improving, if slowly, but the Sydney Harbour Bridge had finally been opened, amid huge outpourings of community pride, on Saturday 19 March. On the same day, at Randwick, Ammon Ra beat Nightmarch in the Chipping Norton Stakes.

RACE DAY. Most patrons coming to Agua Caliente from the US preferred to park their cars on their own side of the border, and get to
the track from there. This meant a second or two's delay at Customs
(the wait on the way back was the other side of an hour), followed by
a stroll though some of the poorest, most decrepit parts of North
America. Everywhere, it seemed, were horridly dressed hagglers,
some as young as five or six, selling whatever trinkets or culinary
delights they could muster. And tickets to the track. A bank of taxis
awaited the pilgrims from the north, some going to downtown
Tijuana, but most to the course, through poorly paved roads or via
shortcuts along narrow, crowded alleyways. 'Everything was dry,
dusty and dirty,' wrote one American racegoer, Ron Hale, of his experience at Agua Caliente years later. 'You could see wooden shacks
clear up into the foothills. Everywhere were small swirls of smoke
from fires built to burn garbage. Clothes hung from makeshift
clotheslines . . . and everywhere were small, poorly clad children with
seemingly nothing to do and nowhere to go.'

Then, turn one more corner and there was the Agua Caliente
grandstand, out of place, colossal. Between 15,000 and 25,000
excited race fans (some reports, including Bert Wolfe's, put the
crowd as high as 50,000, the official attendance as a record 18,000,
but many sneaked in without paying) would arrive this day, to wit-
ness arguably Phar Lap's greatest win.

In Australia, there was much debate about the field opposed to
Phar Lap, with many critics dismissing its quality. They pointed out
that the race would be held far away from the main centres of US
racing in the east. Elliott would later admit that the standard of
racing in California was clearly below that of Sydney and Melbourne.
Most of the American cracks were being aimed at big races later in
the year, so an event in late March did not really fit their programs.
And although David Davis might have been happy to bring his star all
the way from Braeside, many US trainers saw a return journey west

and the primitive sanitary conditions in Mexico as being too hard an ask on their charges. Consequently, the two biggest stars of the American turf—the Kentucky Derby winner, Twenty Grand, and his great rival, Mate—and a number of other topliners declined invitations to run at Agua Caliente.

However, at least some of Phar Lap's rivals had impressive résumés. Phar Lap was top weight, with 9.3. Closest to him in the weights, at 8.8, was Doctor Freeland who would break down during the race; he was a former Preakness Stakes winner. Reveille Boy had won an American Derby, albeit at tote odds of 55–1, but Gallant Knight, which ran second in that race, also ran second to Gallant Fox in the Kentucky Derby. After winning a rich one-mile handicap in New Orleans on 20 February, Spanish Play, the Louisiana Derby winner, was rated by his owner as being 'about the fifth best horse in America'. Even so, it was none of this trio who challenged the Australian for favouritism. Instead two three-year-olds—Cabezo, whose best form was over shorter distances, and Joe Flores—moved to the second line of betting.

The horses were numbered in barrier order, so Phar Lap was No. 9 in a field of eleven. His injured hoof was encased in adhesive tape, with rubber bands wrapped around. In the crowd was a cross-section of movie stars and other celebrities. Al Jolson had sung at the casino the night before, and would do so again that night. Buster Keaton was there, as was Eddie Cantor, Wallace Beery and a collection of ravishing blonde starlets.

Bert Wolfe: Elliott was very nervous and said, 'I hope to goodness that I do the right thing in the race.' Woodcock replied, 'You can't do the wrong thing, because he'll win very easily.'

The start was delayed around twenty minutes, first because the pre-race razzmatazz kept the horses in the mounting yard and then because Reveille Boy, a renowned barrier rogue, refused to go into line. Although this occupied most of his attention, starter Marshal Cassidy kept an eye on the favourite. At one point he yelled at Elliott, 'Wake that horse up, I don't want him to go to sleep.' To which Elliott replied, 'He'll come to life soon enough.' Reveille Boy was eventually shifted to the outside of the field and then condescended to move up.

Tommy Woodcock: He (Billy Elliott) had too tight a hold of him at the barrier, and as they started, the horse went up in the air a little bit. The first 'round past the stand he was that wide I thought, 'Where are you going to go?' I thought he was going to go over the outside fence on him. Aw, he was off the course, and when he went 'round the turn I think there was only one horse behind him. By Joves, though, it was dusty.

Billy Elliott: He was one of the last away, and was slightly cut off by three other horses outside, but I had planned to take the horse to the outside and give him plenty of room, which I did, racing in the centre of the track for the first two furlongs. Rounding the first turn, the horse was inclined to throw his head up, owing to dirt from the flying hoofs hitting him on the head; so I took him out very wide until reaching the back stretch, when I allowed him to race at top speed, and how did he gallop!

The Lexington Thoroughbred Record: It was midway of the backstretch that Phar Lap made his move. Jockey W. Elliott, who had been restraining him in confident fashion, sent him forward and he came from sixth place to obtain a three lengths lead before the turn was reached. Once in front, Elliott took him in hand, and when Reveille Boy made a bold challenge at the stretch turn had enough in hand to draw away and win easily. Truly a superhorse is Phar Lap. Reveille Boy had made many friends by his showing, and his challenge at the stretch turn was a gem of equine courage. Headed by a superior horse, Reveille Boy fought gallantly to gain command, but Phar Lap was too much for him and drew away. Scimitar was the surprise horse. Recently claimed for a nominal sum, the former Tijuana Cup winner ran the best race of his career to be a game third.

Tommy Woodcock: Along the back stretch was two furlongs, and when he got 'round the turn and straightened up, gee, Billy let him go and he went from second last to first in two furlongs, and he got far enough in front to get on the fence before the other turn. And, of course, the other turn was the two-furlong turn 'round into the straight and the run home. So, anyhow, Billy used him up a fair bit, and when he got on the fence he eased him up a bit. Coming 'round the home turn a horse reined up about half a length behind him and stopped with him for a few strides. Elliott had a pretty firm hold on him, but the last furlong he just clicked him up and let him go, and he just streaked away and he won by two or three lengths.

R.E. Leighninger (turf correspondent for The New York Press): Phar Lap did just exactly what his Australian friends said he would do. He ran the race just as they described it in advance. In the mile-and-a-quarter journey, to my way of thinking, Phar Lap ran at top speed [for only] one-sixteenth of a mile. That was between the six-furlong pole and the five-and-a-half chute on the side. There, far out in the middle of the track, where no horse could bother him, he went forward with the speed of an express train . . .

After opening up his commanding lead, Phar Lap was taken under hard restraint by jockey Elliott. He let the others gain on him, notably Reveille Boy. Thousands in the stand thought Reveille Boy was challenging him at the top of the stretch. Jockey Wholey, who rode Reveille Boy, thought the same thing. But Wholey found to his sorrow that Phar Lap was only kidding him.

Elliott didn't even find it necessary to go to a hand ride. Wholey said the boy on Phar Lap simply made a light hissing sound to Phar Lap and away he went—leaving Reveille Boy—to win as he pleased. Phar Lap was in reality only cantering at the finish. The boy had eased him up soon after he passed the eighth pole.

Johnny Longden (the great American jockey who rode the three-year-old Bahamas): To tell you the truth, I had no chance to see where Phar Lap was. The chart record of the race reports him as having run his six furlongs over near the outer rail, his jockey being cautious against any chance of being caught in a speed jam. The next thing I heard was the announcer saying, 'There goes Phar Lap, taking the lead.' From that point on, it was 'Katy, bar the door,' and Phar Lap was home.

David Davis: I am glad the strain is over. I've never felt more excited in my life, not even when Phar Lap won the Melbourne Cup. All the credit is Woodcock's, who trained the horse just as Telford suggested. Phar Lap is the biggest advertisement Australia has ever had . . . I was never in any doubt as to the outcome. Phar Lap showed today that he is a great horse. He will go after other rich American stakes and I am sure he will be the world's largest money winner before he returns to Australia.

There was pandemonium in the stands when Phar Lap dashed to the lead down the back straight, and the crowd's roars continued unabated all the way to the finish. After the race, he was paraded in front of the main grandstand, and an attempt was made to drape a huge horseshoe of flowers over his neck. But Phar Lap would have none of it, rearing backwards, and eventually the roses were placed around the shoulders of Woodcock, Davis, Elliott, Nielsen and

Martin instead. When the jubilant jockey was finally allowed to leap out of the saddle, he grabbed at the course announcer's microphone and yelled, 'Hello, Australia! Hello, Mother! Your last letter spurred me on. This is a great victory!'

Phar Lap stood tired and curious through it all, ears pricked at all the strange sounding voices, agitated only when they had approached him with that ghastly floral tribute. (Later, Woodcock revealed that the horse had hurt himself when climbing away from the garland.) Before he could lead Phar Lap away and savour his achievement, officials brought the Australian contingent together, to lock arms and offer a 'Cooee' shout for the cameras clicking all around them.

That night, Al Jolson was again the main act at the casino. Reflecting on the day's events, he sang a quick parody of 'It's a Long Way to Tipperary'.

It's a long way to Caliente,
It's a long way to go.
It's a long way across the ocean,
For the richest prize I know.

Goodbye Doctor Freeland,
So long, Spanish Play.
It's a long, long way to Caliente,
But Phar Lap knows the way!

ALTHOUGH SOME CONTEMPORARY reports suggest that Phar Lap coped brilliantly with the Agua Caliente race, Bert Wolfe reckoned he looked 'spent' afterwards. Woodcock was concerned, and said privately that Phar Lap's condition reminded him of how the horse was straight after the C.M. Lloyd Stakes twelve months before. He resolved immediately to give him a short let-up before he raced again. But for Davis it was out-a-there. Phar Lap was not allowed to rest and the very next day he left Mexico by motor float for San Francisco, stopping very infrequently on the way. It was rumoured that this getaway was prompted by Davis' trepidation that the Mexican Government might tax the big cheque in his coat pocket. Whatever the reason, the party made a strangely hurried departure.

Back in Sydney there was regret only in the fact that the race commentary had not been transmitted successfully. An expert from Amalgamated Wireless explained that the time of day was not favourable for such long distance broadcasts, 'because the sun was at its zenith between Australia and the United States'. The voice of George Schilling, a respected American race steward who had the job that day as commentator, was heard at irregular intervals, but so frequently did the line drop out that it was impossible to piece together an accurate picture of the race. At one point, though, listeners heard Schilling shout, 'Come on, you beauty! Come on!' which seemed to indicate that the favourite was home.

Among a bevy of opinions, Jim Pike was asked by journalists for his thoughts. 'Just what I expected of him,' he replied, 'as long as he was all right. Now he can go on against the best and they won't beat him. His trainer has the laugh on them for criticising his training of Phar Lap, who was worked no differently than in Australia.'

Meanwhile, ensconced in San Francisco, Davis was sifting though a wide range of offers. Among his horse's suitors were various race-club secretaries and Hollywood producers. Woodcock told him that the horse's leg was not too serious, although he would need a let-up and he did seem a little listless. Perhaps then, movies before match races. Then his secretary brought in another telegram, this one carrying a special seal . . .

Heartiest congratulations on great victory of Phar Lap, George V

'I think I'll have it photographed. Thank you,' Davis said to Wolfe when he showed him the telegram as soon after as possible. 'Maybe I should be taking the horse to England.' Twenty-four hours later, the story of the telegram was front-page news across Australia. From Kentucky came a comment from Colonel Matt Winn, for thirty-three years the director of the Kentucky Derby and best in the game at organising match races, who reckoned Phar Lap was to racing what Babe Ruth was to baseball and Jack Dempsey to boxing. 'The invasion of Phar Lap and his victory at Agua Caliente has stirred the imagination of every race fan,' he said. A clash between Twenty Grand and Phar Lap will be a beauty. Joe MacLennan, secretary of the Southern Maryland Agricultural Association (which conducted racing at the Bowie track in Baltimore), remarked, 'We consider Phar Lap the greatest attraction on the American turf today ... Personally, I believe every turf enthusiast from Maine to California would like to see this great wonder horse perform.' Davis was not short of options.

Publicly, the Phar Lap camp was ultra-positive, and on 4 April Davis flew to Los Angeles to discuss his cinematic options, which apparently included a $100,000 proposal from Metro Goldwyn Meyer for a series of short films in which Phar Lap was to star. However, privately there were sufficient concerns for Davis, in a cable to his business partner in Sydney, Mr L.M. Morris, to say that the champion was 'not himself'. When Woodcock was woken early on the morning or 5 April, California time, by a horse who was clearly extremely distressed, their worries had become genuine fears.

WEDNESDAY 6 APRIL 1932 was going to be a busy day for all staff on the afternoon papers around Australia. The hearing in which the

High Court had been asked to rule on the validity of part of the Financial Agreements Enforcement Act—legislation that had been introduced by the just-elected Lyons Federal Government but was now being challenged by New South Wales premier Jack Lang—was about to conclude in Sydney. The general consensus among political commentators was that unless the High Court upheld the challenge the Lang Government was doomed. But Lang would go down fighting, everyone knew that. Whatever the outcome a major political crisis in New South Wales was imminent.

At 10.30 a.m. the verdict was delivered—a vote of four to two in favour of the Commonwealth—a major political news story with colossal ramifications for the entire community. At *The Sun* in Sydney the reaction was immediate. Prepared headlines were swung into action and the paper was on the street at 10.37 heralding the story as its page-one lead. An astonishing achievement. They'd probably even beaten the wirelesses!

In much smaller type but also on page one, in the Stop Press, was a shocking tale, if true. Unconfirmed cables from California had reported that Phar Lap was dead, cause of death unknown, in fact all details unknown. Sub-editors and printers who for one brief moment had been patting themselves on the back for their special High Court edition were now straight back to work. Urgent clarification was sought. Bert Wolfe's scoop had been picked up by the office of the Melbourne *Herald* around 10 a.m. Immediately the wire had been sent on to Sydney, stressing that the story had not been corroborated, that they were awaiting further news. But confirmation quickly followed, and by 10.48 a second edition of *The Sun* was on the streets, with no change to the High Court story but with the news 'PHAR LAP DEAD!' a feature of the Stop Press section.

By lunchtime *The Sun* was fielding hundreds of calls from readers wanting more information. How could this happen? Was it accident or murder? Someone must be responsible? Across Australia and in New Zealand too large crowds gathered outside the offices of all the major newspapers, as they had done in the pre-radio days to 'watch' the Melbourne Cup, get the latest Test cricket scores or discover seat-by-seat election results. For its main afternoon edition, *The Sun* carried two page-one leads: 'HIGH COURT VERDICT FAVORS LYONS' and, complete with photograph, 'PHAR LAP'S MYSTERY DEATH'.

Later in the day, in Bathurst, as the Prime Minister was surrounded by reporters, the first question he was asked was not about his High Court victory, but about the death of a racehorse.

The Death

Following his Agua Caliente triumph, Phar Lap had been floated to the property of prominent racer and breeder, Edward D. Perry. Perry had forty-four acres at Menlo Park in Atherton, 32 kilometres south of San Francisco and 16 kilometres from Tanforan Racetrack at San Bruno. The champion was led to the No.3 box, which had a sliding door with a 90-centimetre opening protected by a steel-mesh screen between the top of the door and the roof. Nielsen, Elliott and Martin slept in the rooms above Phar Lap's stall, while Woodcock was quartered closer still, across the walkway from the horse.

On the fateful morning of 5 April, after Nielsen medicated a distressed Phar Lap, he departed to find the Tanforan racecourse vet, Caesar Masoero. At some stage, he also took time to telephone Bert Wolfe in San Francisco to tell him of Phar Lap's illness. By mid-afternoon the biggest racing story in memory was buzzing across the Pacific Ocean. 'HE IS DEAD' declared the headline boards of Melbourne's afternoon Herald, and the front page announced:

PHAR LAP DEAD ... CHAMPION HORSE DIES OF ENTERITIS

Menlo Park, California—Tuesday, 3.48 p.m.:

Phar Lap, the Australian champion racehorse, died today.

Dr Nielsen, the Australian veterinary surgeon, conducted an autopsy and certified that death was due to acute enteritis. He and Dr Caesar Masoero, of San Francisco, found that the stomach was highly inflamed and perforated, and agreed that the fatal illness had begun at least two days before the horse's death.

Dr Nielsen said that he believed that alfalfa or barley covered with dew in the stable yard had been eaten by Phar Lap and had caused poisoning because it was not properly prepared. [Early messages gave the cause of death as colic and indigestion] ...

Mr Nielsen called in other veterinary surgeons, who worked hard, but they were unable to overcome the impaction (lodgment in the intestines).

Rumours spread all over America that the horse had been poisoned, but these were immediately emphatically discounted by Dr Nielsen, Woodcock and Elliott.

To remove all suspicion, Frank Love, police chief of Menlo Park, and Edward Farrell, police chief of Atherton, announced today that they would have Phar Lap's oats examined.

Phar Lap died at around 8.30 a.m., Australian eastern standard time, on Wednesday 6 April. For the death and the subsequent developments to be reported in such detail by Australian papers that same afternoon, suspicion, rumour and Bert Wolfe must have all been moving quickly.

IN DEATH, AS IN LIFE, the Phar Lap story was never going to be a straightforward one. Within eight hours, the cause of death had been one or all of colic and indigestion, acute enteritis, poisoning, green feed and 'the impaction'.

'Phar Lap has been poisoned' headlines appeared in Australia and the United States the next day. *The New York Times* on 6 April ran a front-page story headlined: 'PHAR LAP GREAT AUSTRALIAN RACEHORSE DIES IN WEST AFTER FIRST AMERICAN TRIUMPH'. That story confirmed the US opinion of the champion and reported the circulation of rumours about the cause of death. Developments unfolded in newspapers around the world.

Melbourne's *Sun News-Pictorial* had a 'special correspondent' in California who reported, 'Dr Nielsen told me by telephone that the lining of the horse's stomach was inflamed and that the coating had been eaten off as if by an irritant.' At the same time, *The Sydney Morning Herald* carried a series of stories which indicated that, even in the Phar Lap camp, persistent rumours were causing second thoughts. First, the paper reported:

Vancouver, 6 April: Discounting rumours of the poisoning of Phar Lap, Mr Davis said that the first findings attributing death to colic had been definitely accepted. After conferring with the jockey, W. Elliott, he said that there would be no further inquiry. He admitted that the trip from Australia might have weakened the horse . . .

However, *The Sydney Morning Herald* also suggested that later in the day Mr Davis said:

I cannot conceive of any fiend who might have been vicious enough to poison Phar Lap, but I have never heard of a horse dying from colic just the way that Phar Lap did. I believe I owe it to other horsemen to make a thorough examination. There is also the chance that he may have been poisoned accidentally, and if that is the case we want to know about it.

So Davis, after asking the advice of Billy Elliott, a fair jockey with an excellent record on Phar Lap but unknown veterinary qualifications, concluded that colic was the cause of death. Soon after, Davis, drawing on his experience of having been present at the death from colic of an unknown number of horses, believed that Phar Lap's was an unusual case and thus the prospect of the horse being poisoned warranted further investigations.

Poisoning is inflammatory, both biologically and journalistically. Wolfe referred to 'poisoning' having been caused by oats or alfalfa as the cause of death. Police investigation of 'poisoning' was related to the introduction of some substance not normally part of the equine diet. In the days that followed, the search for an explanation crystallised into three key areas of investigation—colic, malicious poisoning and accidental poisoning.

COLIC IS AN INTESTINAL DISTURBANCE that can occur for a number of reasons or for no reason at all. In colic, rhythmical, painful contractions of the muscular wall of the stomach and intestines cause the horse to paw the ground with its forefeet, to kick at its stomach with its hind legs, and to get down and lie on its side or back. Such activity can result in a strangling of the intestines leading to rupture and death. Colic can be caused by a bowel obstruction, where a blockage of the intestine by food occurs. The fermentation of green feed in the stomach and intestines can also cause colic: fermentation causes a build-up of gas pressure, colic is experienced and, if the pressure is not relieved, eventually the stomach or intestines rupture, or the horse succumbs to the secondary effects on other organs of the internal pressure.

Police investigations centred on the possibility of intentional administration of a poison to Phar Lap. Although it was possible, with as many as 1500 people visiting Phar Lap the previous day to see what the Agua Caliente propagandists had called the 'Anzac Antelope', there seemed to be little evidence of it.

In an article published in The Sporting Globe in 1936, ostensibly as told to the journalist J.M. Rohan by Tommy Woodcock but apparently not in his words, Woodcock claimed to have spoken with a gangster called 'The Brazilian' when Woodcock was training for

Willis Kilmer in the United States. Kilmer was the owner of the world's then leading money earner, Sun Beau, and offered Woodcock a training position after Phar Lap's death. The article claimed the gangster admitted to Woodcock that he had slipped something to Phar Lap the night before he died 'and I would have put a slug in you if you had woken up while I was there'.

This seems too fanciful to be believed. There are a series of discrepancies in the *Sporting Globe* stories that bring their veracity into question. The best part of fifty years later, in interviews with the author Jan Wositzky, Woodcock said: 'And often I wondered: the vet was out; he used to go out quite a lot. I wonder, early in the morning, maybe he wasn't quite awake or something like that ... could he have mixed up the wrong medicine?'

Given the option in 1985 of repeating his gangster story or appearing disloyal to Nielsen, Woodcock chose the harsher, though seemingly equally unlikely version, further discounting the credibility of the *Sporting Globe* story.

Years after that series was first published, Bill Stutt, a prominent and distinguished racing man all his life, President of the Moonee Valley Racing Club for twenty-five years and for whom Woodcock trained many horses, had a conversation at Woodcock's stables, which he recalled for the authors:

> I never brought the subject up because [I knew] how fond he was of the horse, it saddened him, those things coming back to mind. But one day I was down at the stables and his staff weren't there ... somehow something came up about Phar Lap and it was the first time really he had ever mentioned it, but he started to tell me things and I suppose he talked for about an hour and a half. I remember being absolutely engrossed with what he told me ... When he spoke to me about it, at the stables—he was terribly worked up. He didn't know why he died. I don't think he thought the horse had been poisoned.

One of the chief problems with deliberate-poisoning theories is the lack of motive. Criminal elements allegedly hurt by Davis' betting sting at Agua Caliente would have been much more inclined to strike before the big race than after the champion bolted. More likely, they were quietly planning approaches to Davis, with a variety of get-rich-quick strategies. Local racing interests were hardly likely to kill Phar Lap out of jealousy—he'd already lured a course record crowd to Tijuana and seemed set to do so across the country, giving the sport a kickstart it desperately needed. Anti-racing campaigners in California, who were accused in some quarters of being responsible, were hardly the types to murder an innocent animal to further their cause. But even if forces of evil were at play here, their reputed choice of killer—arsenic, a slow-working poison—could not have caused the dreadful damage that killed Phar Lap.

Inadvertent poisoning was for a long time the prime suspect. On Thursday 31 March, Victor C. Weltzin of Palo Alto had visited the Perry establishment to spray liveoak trees on the western boundary of the ranch. He reportedly used a commercial orchard spray, a lead arsenate compound. He warned ranch hands not to allow stock to feed on the leaves of the sprayed trees. The wind that day was blowing from the west.

After Phar Lap's death an inspector from the Food and Drug Administration of the United States Department of Agriculture was sent to investigate any connection between the tragedy and the spraying. He took samples of liveoak leaves, grass in the paddock adjacent to the sprayed trees and samples of the Australian wheat, bran and chaff and New Zealand oats shipped with the horse. He also sampled some clay balls and the bedding straw from the horse's stall.

Australian readers, hungry for any information that might unravel the mystery, read on 8 April a report that began: 'A chemical examination of the stomach of Phar Lap will be made, it was announced today by the veterinary surgeon, Dr William Nielsen, who said that the stomach and the intestines would be taken to the laboratory of the Hooper Foundation for Medical Research at the University of California …' Then a cable the following day said, 'A Government official declared that an inspection of Phar Lap's organs revealed that he was poisoned by spray used on the trees on March 31, which drifted onto grass which the horse ate.'

For four days, there was merely conjecture. Then, under the headline 'Phar Lap's Death', came two reports in *The Sydney Morning Herald*:

Montreal, 13 April: A United Press message from San Francisco says that chemists and toxicologists pursuing separate inquiries regarding Phar Lap have advanced conflicting opinions as to the cause of death. Chemists at the University of California reported to Mr D.J. Davis, part-owner of the horse, that a small amount of arsenic was found in the analysis of the internal organs, but it was not sufficient to cause death.

An autopsy by city chemists, the message adds, disclosed that the horse suffered from stomach ulcers, indicating that he was ill before arriving in the United States, and was a sick horse when he won the Agua Caliente Handicap.

San Francisco, 13 April: Mr W.W. Vincent, chief food and drug administrator of the United States Department of Agriculture, who has made an examination, announces that poison commonly used as a tree spray was present in the organs of Phar Lap.

Edward Perry, the owner of the ranch at which the drama unfolded, scoffed at the Food and Drug Administration's claim of death caused by spray, pointing out that, 'Many of my own animals grazed with the Australian "Red Terror", ate of the same grass, and much more of it, but none of them were stricken.'

Finally on 28 April, under the banner 'Phar Lap, Result of Autopsy' this brief paragraph appeared in a number of Australian papers:

San Francisco, 26 April: Chemists, veterinary surgeons, and Federal officials have completed a three weeks' investigation of the death of Phar Lap. They ascribe death to colic and reported that lead arsenate had been found in the vital organs. However, they could not determine whether this caused the fatal attack of acute indigestion. They explained that the quantity was 'very small', indicating the belief that the horse might have survived if he had been otherwise sound.

It is little wonder that Australians remain to this day suspicious of Americans when discussion turns to who killed Phar Lap. It is always who and not what. Various 'officials' and 'experts' had 'investigations' and the conclusions were both contradictory and unconvincing. We can, however, be certain of a few facts.

Vets Nielsen and Masoero (the Tanforan racecourse vet) arrived after Phar Lap died. They performed an autopsy within hours, and copies of their signed statements were sent to Harry Telford by David Davis' representative in Sydney. The reports were eventually published in Smith's Weekly, in Sydney, in April 1935.

I was called at 5.15 a.m. on the 5th April by Mr T. Woodcock to have a look at the racehorse, Phar Lap. The animal showed symptoms of colic and was led out into the paddock. The symptoms at first were not alarming. His pulse was a little increased, but his temperature remained normal. At 11 a.m. he was still in the same condition. At 12 noon his temperature had increased to 102° and the animal showed signs of extreme distress. At this time I diagnosed the condition as one of acute poisoning and hurried in the car to obtain the services of Dr. Masoero.

Whilst I was away the animal succumbed.

POST-MORTEM EXAMINATION

The stomach was inflamed, the large and small bowel severely inflamed, and the liver also showed a general condition of inflammation throughout. The signs present were those of acute gastric enteritis brought about, in my opinion, by some toxic substance, the toxic substance causing same I am unable to say.

Sgd. (Dr.) William M. Nielsen,

Veterinary Surgeon.

On April 5th, about 2.15 p.m., I received a phone call asking me to see the horse Phar Lap. I arrived at Menlo Park about 3.20 p.m. Phar Lap was dead. I found the body distended by internal gas. Dr Nielsen and myself obtained permission from Mr D.J. Davis to open the horse for an autopsy.

Upon opening the stomach I found a very severe inflammation, so was the colon very much inflamed. It is my opinion that he had not eaten anything for at least twelve hours, as all the food was digested. There was no intestinal obstruction.

In my opinion the horse died through some poison substance in his stomach. An ordinary case of colic would not have killed the horse in such a short time. There was about two quarts of digested stuff in his stomach.

Sgd. (Dr.) C. Masoero

Veterinary Surgeon, San Francisco.

The autopsy conducted at the Hooper Foundation at the University of California resulted in the following statement:

Present at the examination on April 9, 1932, of organs of Phar Lap— D.J. Davis, owner; Dr W.M. Nielsen, vet.; T. Woodcock, the trainer; Professor F.T. Green, Dr R.T. Creely, Fire-chief D. Murphy, a representative of the Division of Food and Insecticide Control, U.S.

Department of Agriculture.

\All the organs and tissues were in an advanced state of decomposition. The horse died at 2 p.m., 5/4/32; organs removed 7/4/32.

(Sgd.) Dr. K.F. Meyer

AUTOPSY FINDINGS

An acute stasis of the spleen is regularly observed in cases of fatal colic due to torsion or volvulus of the colon. It is also noted in the course of heart failure, although stasis of the liver accompanies the enlargement of the spleen.

Since the stasis is confined to the spleen it is reasonable to suspect that some profound disturbance in the large intestine or stomach (unfortunately not available for examination) caused the death of the horse.

The gross anatomical observations on the few pieces of intestines, liver and spleen submitted for examination support the antemortium observations.

The horse Phar Lap in all probability suffered from a non-febrile colicky affection and died from the sequelae.

Based on the examination of the organs which were available after the death of Phar Lap in conjunction with detailed chemical analysis conducted by several agencies, the under-signed have come to the conclusion that the death of the racehorse Phar Lap was caused by a colicky condition manifesting itself in the form of an acute inflammation of the stomach and intestines.

An enormous accumulation of gas in the stomach and intestines was principally responsible for the sudden death of the animal. The factors responsible for the acute inflammation have not been determined, and probably will never be determined on account of the incompleteness of the clinical data and post-mortem findings.

To date, lead arsenate which was found in very small quantities in the body of the horse and in the feed may be responsible for the irritation of the intestinal tract.

(Sgd.) T.R. Creely, D.V.S.; Professor Frank Green,

Dr C. Masoero, Dr K.F. Meyer.

The great heart, that physical pump of gargantuan dimensions that symbolises both Phar Lap's superiority as an equine athlete and the courage at the centre of the legend, was sent at Davis' request to Australia. It was examined by Dr Stewart McKay, the veterinarian so fascinated by Phar Lap and his physiology, and Professor Welsh from the University of Sydney. They found that the heart weighed 14 lb (that of an average racehorse weighing 9–10 lb) and the walls of the left ventricle were $1^3/4$ inches thick (compared with an average of one inch).

According to The Sydney Morning Herald of 20 May 1932, Dr McKay said that the heart was perfectly healthy and the great horse certainly did not die from heart disease. An effusion of blood had been discovered under the pericardium (the sac around the heart) but this apparently had not interfered with the health of the heart.

SO WHAT DID KILL PHAR LAP? The racing world needed an explanation for his death. At least four investigations were conducted. None had all the evidence. None had conclusive proof. Best guesses were given as reasons. What is certain is that the champion died a painful, relatively rapid death, that his stomach was distended and that bloody fluid spurted from his nostrils as he died. His stomach was perforated and was perhaps weakened by chronic stomach ulcers, although modern veterinary thought is that stomach ulcers are relatively common in racehorses.

The symptoms do not support poisoning. Analysis of what organs were available showed insufficient evidence of arsenic for that to have been an influence. Professor Frank T. Green, a member of the Hooper Foundation team, analysed samples of liver, lung, spleen, stomach and kidney for 'common volatile poisons, alkaloidal poisons, arsenic and mercury' and found nothing.

Phar Lap's stomach distended as he struggled through that agonising morning. The gas observed by Masoero to be distending the body may have been due to the breakdown of the tissues after death. The speed of Phar Lap's death tells us that something more than colic was responsible. Gas distension from green feed must be considered, yet for Woodcock to have made such a fundamental mistake is so unlikely as to be not credible. And Phar Lap's symptoms and the course of the illness do not support such a diagnosis.

The search was for a smoking gun, but should have been for a time machine. The veterinary profession in 1932 had not discovered the disease that killed Phar Lap.

IN THE YEARS SINCE Phar Lap's death, it has been suggested in some quarters that he may have succumbed to the disease 'Colitis X', a form of peracute colitis of unknown cause. It is an acute inflammation of the caecum and the large colon, its most striking feature the sudden onset of profuse watery diarrhoea. Nowhere in Woodcock's description of that morning is such a symptom mentioned. In fact, he stated later that he and Nielsen inspected Phar Lap's droppings early in the morning and the result of that inspection prompted Nielsen to comment, 'Gee, he don't seem bad.'

According to Dr Sally Church, a senior lecturer in equine medicine and surgery at the University of Melbourne, it is very unlikely that any description of the symptoms of a horse suffering from Colitis X would fail to mention diarrhoea. Having had described to her Phar

Lap's symptoms as reported by Tommy Woodcock, Dr Church was inclined to suggest another disease of uncertain bacterial origin, Duodenitis-Proximal jejunitis (also known as Anterior enteritis) as the likely cause of death.

A very fit racehorse has a circulating blood volume of 30 to 40 litres. Body fluid flows at a rate of 100 litres per day into the horse's intestines and is reabsorbed into the body in the colon. If the fluid is prevented from making its way down the intestinal tract to be reabsorbed, two things happen. First, organs and muscles are starved of fluid and their functioning begins to deteriorate. Second, the stomach and small intestines above the obstruction blocking the path of the fluid become filled to bursting point. The horse experiences severe abdominal pain. The pressure of the fluid inflow will eventually rupture the horse's stomach.

How can this be relevant to Phar Lap's death, as Dr Masoero, who performed the autopsy on the day of the death, said there was no obstruction in the intestine?

THE VERY FIRST REPORT in the *Melbourne Herald*, just eight hours after the champion had died, contained probably the most accurate of all diagnoses reached in the days and weeks following Phar Lap's demise. After the initial autopsy was conducted, Nielsen described the cause of death as an acute enteritis, that is, a severe inflammation of the intestine. He and Masoero both thought the enteritis was caused by a toxic substance, most likely, in their view, a poison. Their only error was in ascribing the source of the toxin: modern veterinary science would suggest the toxin that killed Phar Lap was produced by bacteria.

Veterinary surgeons today know that horses can be quickly killed by Duodenitis-Proximal jejunitis. Even now, however, the disease process is not well understood. It is thought to be caused by one of the family of bacteria *Clostridium*, a family known for its role in botulism and tetanus. It is thought that the bacteria produce a toxin which attacks the lining of the horse's gut, causing a functional obstruction. The walls of the small intestine are severely damaged and acutely inflamed, and cease to function. The intestine is blocked, not by a physical barrier but by a length of intestine which refuses to function. Death is caused by either the gross imbalance in the horse's body fluids causing damage to vital organs, or a rupturing of the stomach.

Woodcock was most likely drenched by stomach contents. This fluid would have been stained with blood and the products of the breakdown of the wall of the intestines and stomach. With the enormous pressure inside the gut built up by the fluid inflow that could not be passed down to the colon for reabsorption, as Phar Lap fell during his death throes some of the stomach contents would inevitably have been forced through his nostrils. The textbook description of Duodenitis-Proximal jejunitis is a list of Phar Lap's symptoms: elevated temperature, increased pulse rate, acute colic, distension of the small intestines, a build up of fluid in the stomach leading to perforation and rapid death. The lining of the gut is destroyed by the toxin produced by the *Clostridium* bacterial infection. When Nielsen and Masoero performed the autopsy, the appearance of the intestines persuaded them that the horse had died of something other than colic. This appearance is entirely consistent with Duodenitis-Proximal jejunitis.

Why did the horse become infected? Stress can make a horse more susceptible than normal to bacterial infections. A change of environment or weather, hard racing, and in particular travel, can cause a horse a great deal of stress. In almost all cases of Duodenitis-Proximal jejunitis, the horse has travelled significant distances in the preceding weeks.

DR JOHN VAN VEENENDAAL graduated as a veterinary surgeon in 1976. He has worked almost all his professional life with performance animals, as a racetrack practitioner and since 1990 as a specialist equine surgeon. During this time he has worked in many great Australian racing stables, including those of Bart Cummings, T.J. Smith, Lee Freedman, Colin Hayes, John Meagher and John Sadler, who between them have trained nineteen Melbourne Cup winners and countless Group One performers. Van Veenendaal also treated some of the horses trained by Tommy Woodcock. Of the subject of this book he says simply, 'I have yet to see a horse perform the way that history tells us Phar Lap did.'

In February 2000, the authors sought his analysis of Phar Lap's death. While the subject of Phar Lap had occasionally been a topic of conversation between Dr van Veenendaal and Woodcock, until now the equine surgeon had never sighted the post mortem reports. This was Dr van Veendenaal's response to our approach:

Thank you for your invitation to express an opinion on the death of Phar Lap.

I knew Tommy Woodcock in my capacity as a referral surgeon. Obviously any chat with Tommy soon turned to the discussions about Phar Lap and his death. From the history and graphic descriptions Tommy related to me, I had formed the opinion that Phar Lap had died of an acute enteric disease, either 'Anterior Enteritis' or 'Colitis X'.

From the reports and post mortem findings you have provided to me, there are several points which can be made:

1. The post mortem lesions were confined mainly to the upper intestinal tract, with little colonic involvement, therefore ruling out Colitis X as a possibility.

2. The gastric ulceration that is featured in these reports is probably an incidental finding. Gastric ulceration in racing thoroughbreds is a very common condition and reflects the high grain, concentrated diets that they are fed.

3. The arsenicals found in the vital organs would not have been an unusual finding. In those times, many thoroughbreds were given tonics containing arsenicals, notably 'Fowlers Solution'.

4. Phar Lap did die of poisoning but not a poison that was given maliciously or intentionally. The poison was an enterotoxin that caused Anterior Enteritis or more correctly Duodenitis-Proximal jejunitis. The clinical features that Tommy described to me and the reports that you have supplied me with indicate that this was the most probable cause of death.

In my experience as a racetrack practitioner and a referral surgeon I have seen numerous cases of Duodenitis-Proximal jejunitis. The consistent findings are fever, acute abdominal pain with rapid deterioration to depression and, without intensive supportive therapy, death from enterotoxic shock, severe dehydration and respiratory compromisation from acute distention of the stomach and upper small intestines. Physical obstructions or strangulations of the small intestine usually do not deteriorate as rapidly nor do they have a fever. The salient words in William Nielsen's report on the post mortem examination are: 'The signs present were those of acute gastric enteritis brought about, in my opinion, by some toxic substance, the toxic substance causing same I am unable to say.'

The disease syndrome, now known as Duodenitis-Proximal jejunitis was not described in the literature until the early 1980s. Nielsen would not have been aware of this disease but his summation of the cause of death was correct.

Despite the diagnostic techniques and treatment options available today, Duodenitis-Proximal jejunitis kills close to 70 per cent of horses stricken by it. Phar Lap had no chance. The disease had not been discovered in April 1932, so it was never considered as a possible cause of the taking of a hero. As the disease was unknown, so was the treatment. Phar Lap's death was tragically premature and painfully sudden. No amount of care could have prevented it; no skill would have stopped it.

Epilogue

Andrew Barton 'Banjo' Paterson was the editor of the Sydney weekly, The Sydney Sportsman—a paper that devoted most of its pages to racing—from 1922 to 1930 and from not long afterwards a regular and witty racing correspondent with *The Sydney Mail*. Inevitably, he was a close and passionate observer of Phar Lap, of whom he once wrote, 'Of course, there is Phar Lap, the one and only, a freak, a horse of the century.'

'The public will stand paying their money to see Phar Lap win his races in exercise canters,' the Banjo wrote with an eye for history when others were suggesting that the great horse was ruining racing. 'For Phar Lap is a freak and the rising generation, now growing up, will be proud to say in after years that they saw Phar Lap race. He will become an even greater tradition than Carbine.'

Paterson, of course, was a superb writer, with an immaculate sense of now at a time when racing scribes seemed locked in the past. He appreciated Australians better than most and knew a scoop when he saw one, and clearly had developed an army of contacts, including some in the Telford camp. When many journalists were trying to determine whether Phar Lap would run in the 1931 Caulfield Cup, Paterson told his readers that the stable had instead bet heavily on the Vigne/Phar Lap double. Not long after, responding to the view that Telford had an obligation to reveal his Melbourne Cup hand, he wrote the following for *The Sydney Mail*:

In theatrical parlance the 'gods' are the immortals who sit up aloft in the gallery and make or mar the success of a play. You can fool the intelligentsia with press reviews, but you can't fool the gods. On the turf the gods are the small punters who make up the bulk of a racing attendance, and who become extremely vocal when things do not go exactly to suit them. The gods have been very much concerned with Mr H.R. Telford, trainer and part-owner of the sensational Phar Lap; the gods wanted to know why Telford was so long in declaring his intentions regarding Phar Lap and the Melbourne Cup. The question whether Phar Lap is to run in the Melbourne Cup may be decided by the time that this appears; but even if it is decided the question still remains, should an owner or a trainer ever take the public into his confidence?

Phar Lap is not only a racehorse—he is a business, and a very profitable and important business at that. Phar Lap, Unlimited. For the past three years this business has returned an average profit of over £14,000 a year, which, it must be admitted, is a very satisfactory dividend on an original capital of somewhere about £300. Telford's task, then, has been to see that the plant and machinery of the business as embodied in the racehorse Phar Lap, are used to the best advantage, and are not subjected to undue risks or to anything that might strain or injure their future earning capacity. The problem is not, perhaps, as easy as it looks to the uninitiated.

From the time that Phar Lap won the 1930 Melbourne Cup, a debate began in racing circles as to who was better—Carbine or Phar Lap. Before that Cup, it had been sacrilegious to compare the two.

Sure, Phar Lap was as good as any other champion of the Australian turf, probably better, but never was he to be spoken of in the same breath as Carbine. In the lead-up to the 1930 Cup, in fact from the time Phar Lap, as a three-year-old, smashed the Australasian record in the AJC Plate, the defenders of Carbine—of which there were many—said let's see what he does as a four-year-old. But then Phar Lap won the Cup with 9.12, which had the new champion's admirers asking, 'Wasn't your "Old Jack" beaten in the 1889 Cup as a four-year-old, carrying 10 stone?'

'Ah, well, yes he was,' the old-timers stuttered, before, composure rediscovered, they reminded the Phar Lap supporters about Carbine's amazing Cup win in 1890, lugging 10.5 to victory with a badly cracked hoof as part of a field of thirty-nine. 'Let's see how Phar Lap goes as a five-year-old, that'll prove it.'

Many long-time observers, from the Chairman of the VRC down, were strong supporters of Carbine. In December 1931, Banjo Paterson took a more modern view:

I am often asked whether I think Carbine was better than Phar Lap, who has just gone to America. Of course, it is only one man's opinion but I think the class of horses here improved about 40 per cent with the importation of the stallions Valais and Magpie, and I think the horses all round now are much better than they were then. I saw Carbine run a lot of his races and no doubt he was a great horse, but a horse called Abercorn, that you never hear of nowadays, beat Carbine three times out of seven races and there was very little between them at weight-for-age. If Carbine was a phenomenon then there were two phenomenons at the one time and it doesn't seem very probable.

Marvel beat Carbine at a mile at weight-for-age, and you don't see them beating Phar Lap at weight-for-age. We sent a good many horses to race in England in those days and some of them like Paris, Merman and The Grafter won good handicaps, but we never sent a horse up to English weight-for-age form. If Phar Lap can win in America at weight-for-age, it will put Australia on the turf map for the first time, like the old cricketers and scullers. You younger people that saw Phar Lap race here will be able to say when you get old, 'Ah, don't talk to me about racehorses. You ought to have seen Phar Lap.'

That's about the only advantage a man gets from growing old. He can tell the young fellows they don't know anything.

Four months later, Phar Lap was dead. During his brief life, he'd epitomised the battling 'she'll be right' spirit of working class Australia, an optimism that was sorely tested in the early 1930s. That, perhaps, was his greatest legacy—that he reminded all Australians, even in those grim economic times, whatever their temporary hardship, there *was* hope. Phar Lap was a cheap, awkward horse who'd slaughtered rivals that had cost the aristocracy thousands of pounds. He'd conquered America, or at least was about to. He was brave, having overcome a pauper's start, handicappers, gangsters, even the Pacific Ocean, before—as folklore quickly had it—he died a hero's death. From April 1932, Australians who showed considerable pluck or courage, on the battlefield or the sporting field, were said to 'have a heart as big as Phar Lap'. With all of this, he was the ultimate champion. In all the years since, no Australasian galloper—not Peter Pan, Bernborough, Rising Fast, Tulloch, Kingston Town or Sunline—has been popularly rated his equal.

Still, we can ponder the mountains that Phar Lap might have climbed had he survived the stresses of the Agua Caliente adventure. In the second week of April 1932, as debate raged as to what or who might have killed him, this was what preoccupied Banjo Paterson.

We are told by the poet that, 'Of all the words of tongue or pen, The saddest are "it might have been"', and we are left to speculate on what might have been if Phar Lap had lived long enough to test himself against the best of the Americans.

American opinion, as expressed after the horse's death, was that he would have beaten the best of their horses. Baron Long, for instance, one of the most experienced of the American racing authorities, said that he had seen all the best horses of the world for the past 20 years, but had only seen one Phar Lap. Allowance, however, must be made for his natural desire to say something comforting in our affliction, and the sentiment which is best expressed in the words *de mortuis nil nisi bonum*. We appreciate his testimony, but we have to make allowances for the circumstances. He could hardly have stood by the horse's grave and told us that the horse was no good.

Nor can we make any claim to world supremacy on Phar Lap's Agua Caliente win. Admittedly, the Australian champion was favourably handicapped and he met a field that was reckoned to be below the average for the race—though it could not have been so very far below it, for it contained a winner of a couple of classics. Any advantage that our horse had in the weights, however, was offset by his ridiculously short preparation after a long sea voyage, and the fact that even that preparation was interfered with by an accident to a hoof.

Weighing the evidence as impartially as possible, the balance of testimony, as the lawyers say, is all in favour of the idea that Phar Lap would have gone east and cleaned up the best of the Americans, such as Twenty Grand and Mate, without much trouble. Alas! that he was denied the chance of doing so. We had nothing within stones of him, and it is doubtful whether the Americans had anything within pounds of him. This, of course, is an ex parte statement by an

Australian about an Australian horse, and would be met in America by the national expression of doubt contained in the words, 'Oh, yeah?'—but there is a certain amount of unprejudiced expert opinion to be obtained if we look into the matter.

The production of high-class thoroughbred horses has been a lifelong hobby with the wealthiest men in all parts of the world. No expense has been too severe, no trouble has been too great, to prevent them getting the best, irrespective of nationality; and yet we find that the Continental breeders—French, Germans, Russians, etc.—have unanimously passed over the American performers in favour of the English. The Americans have led the world in motor cars and motion pictures, but they have never led it in horses.

After the defeats of Epinard and Papyrus in the United States, one would have expected a worldwide swing in favour of American stock; but the Russians, French, Germans, Italians, etc., who are not exactly fools, went on buying English horses. Our own share in the contest for world supremacy for breeding racehorses must be classed as negligible, for we never had the money to compete for the best animals. It was just a sheer fluke that a cheap English horse, Night Raid, sired this wonderful chestnut giant, Phar Lap. Such a thing might not happen again for a century, but it happened in our time, and the sorrow of it is that we never saw the question of Australian–American supremacy fully decided ...

Considering the wealth of the Americans and the huge stakes that are given to encourage their breeders, we could hardly expect to beat them with any normal horse; but they are not so far ahead of us to be utterly unbeatable, and a freak like Phar Lap might easily have beaten the best of them.

By Night Raid out of Entreaty

Putting the right price on the head of a yearling—in Phar Lap's case only one year, three months and three weeks after birth—when nothing is known about the existence of qualities that determine the horse's success, is the decision which makes fools of kings and princes of paupers.

Yearling buyers are purchasing hope. Before a bid is made, five generations of pedigree are dissected at length. Horses are removed from boxes to have their walk examined more closely than any super-model's. Straightness of knee, kindness of eye and width of jowl are noted in the margin of the catalogue. The racing records of sisters, cousins and aunts-third-removed all have a bearing on the price an optimistic purchaser may pay. But a young horse knows nothing of the racetrack. Girth strap and saddle are as foreign to a yearling as Plato and Shakespeare. Leg speed, endurance and competitive urge are untested, invisible and often absent, so great emphasis is put on breeding. However, a pedigree is merely a statement of probabilities. If an Oaks-winning mare has a foal by a Derby winner which won a Golden Slipper, a Cox Plate and the Melbourne and Caulfield Cup double, and the foal has four legs and one head, as a yearling its price in the sales ring will be astronomical. It is more likely to be a better racehorse than the son of a country miler out of a city midweek placegetter, but the outcome is never guaranteed. It may also ulti-mately be the world's most expensive show hack. Expensive yearlings are bought when somebody is influenced by probabilities arising from generalities and thus puts a specific expectation on an individual outcome. Such people can share stories with those who put the house on the toss of a coin.

Genetics is so perverse, so dependent on chance, that the identical breeding of two individuals will equally likely result in peas of a pod or ends of a pole. If we look to our human experience, how different can two brothers be, and yet sometimes how much the same? Tommy Woodcock spent three years looking after a horse trained by Harry Telford and thought Harry a hard man. En route to the United States at the end of 1931, Woodcock and Phar Lap stayed with Harry's brother Hugh in New Zealand for five weeks. In Jan Wositzky's collection of interviews with Tommy, Woodcock described this time: 'I had a beautiful time in New Zealand. I stayed with Hughie Telford; a long way different man to Harry. You wouldn't think they was brothers— different training methods. Oh, he was really a peach of a man.'

With genetics such an unreliable aid, purchasers fall back upon appearance. This is why, when hope takes over from reason at the sale ring, a further bid of $5000 can be justified because 'the colt is such a beautiful walker'.

The price of a stallion, on the other hand, is decided in the cold light of a racing record, and there are some legendary stallions in Phar Lap's pedigree. Their combined genetic weight tipped the balance of probabilities in favour of Harry Telford and his ugly duckling.

The three most important influences were Musket, St Simon and Stockwell. Musket was the sire of Carbine, Australia's greatest racehorse of the nineteenth century and, on his return to the UK, a significant stallion. Musket was bred by Lord Glasgow in 1867. Lord Glasgow died in 1869 and his stud went to General Peel and George Payne: they divided the string and Musket went to Payne. Unplaced in two runs as a two-year-old, as a three-year-old he won a number of races over two miles including the Flying Dutchman Handicap. He ultimately won up to three miles. His last race was the two-mile Alexandra Plate at Ascot which he won carrying 9.6. Though a stout stayer, he did not have a spectacular career at stud and was exported to New Zealand in 1878.

St Simon was one of the greatest sires of thoroughbred breeding and also the outstanding stayer of his day. Superlatives are always used when referring to him. He was bred by Prince Batthyany of Hungary, who died in April 1883 in the grandstand at Newmarket. The Prince was on his way to eat in the Jockey Club luncheon room and was anticipating watching his Galliard, a son of his beloved Galopin, run as favourite in the Two Thousand Guineas. The excitement of both was too much for his weak heart. Galliard won, and because of the Prince's demise was sold with the rest of the stable. St Simon, also a son of Galopin, was sold in the dispersal to the Duke of Portland, a man of little means who had inherited the title and one of the greatest fortunes in England from an eccentric second cousin he had never met. He took up racing in 1880, and fortunately asked Mat Dawson, a Scot with a fine feel for horses, to train for him.

Galopin won the Derby, was not entered in the St Leger and did not race as a four-year-old because of concern for Prince Batthyany's constitution. Galopin slowly developed a reputation as a stallion and was champion sire three times. St Simon's dam was St Angela, by King Tom, winner of a pair of Goodwood Cups and runner-up in the Derby. St Angela was sixteen when she foaled St Simon and until that time had been an undistinguished broodmare.

Peter Willott described St Simon in his book, *An Introduction to the Thoroughbred*:

He stood 15 hands, $3^{1}/4$ inches as a three-year-old but grew to 16 hands while he was a stud. So perfectly proportioned that many observers took him to be smaller than he really was. He had great quality and exceptionally concave profile. Shoulders so sloped that he appeared to be short in the back and remarkable length from hip to hock. Observers were equally impressed by his innate vitality and by his action. He was described variously as moving like a greyhound and as if made of elastic. St Simon was prone to irritability and free sweating, and passed on these tendencies to many of his progeny. He also transmitted his good looks and constitution, and much of his superb speed and stamina. His stock were known for being exceptionally clean winded. His sons and daughters needed little work to get them fit and most of them were wonderful movers.

St Simon ran in four races as a two-year-old, including the Prince of Wales Nursery at Doncaster, where he carried the top weight of 9 stone and beat a strong field including St Medard, runner-up in the following year's Two Thousand Guineas. After that race, St Simon was galloped against two other two-year-olds in Dawson's stable, Harvester and Busybody. St Simon beat them so easily that Dawson became concerned with the quality of the two vanquished horses. His fears were unfounded, as the next year Harvester dead-heated in the Derby with St Gatien and Busybody won the Oaks. St Simon then competed in a match race against the Duke of Westminster's two-year-old, Duke of Richmond. St Simon won convincingly and Dawson reputedly said, 'That is the best two-year-old I have ever seen.'

St Simon's first appearance as a three-year-old was in a 'trial match' against the six-year-old Tristan, winner of the Ascot Gold Cup. There was no trophy and no prize money, and two other horses took part to ensure a true pace, but the match was accorded the status of a race as it was recorded in the Racing Calendar. St Simon won easily, by six lengths.

St Simon was given a walkover in the Epsom Gold Cup and won

the Ascot Gold Cup, beating Tristan by twenty lengths. He won a mile cup at Gosforth Park and the Goodwood Cup over two and a half miles by twenty lengths in his final appearance.

The third important sire influence in Phar Lap's pedigree is Stockwell. A champion galloper called The Baron won a St Leger and was mated with the outstanding broodmare Pocahontas to produce two great brothers, Stockwell in 1849 and Rataplan the following year. Stockwell, according to Chiron in *The Australasian*:

> Was a grandly made chestnut, with a streaked face and two white socks behind. He had the reputation of being a plain looking horse and an indifferent mover in his slow paces. He was splendidly proportioned and I have seen him described as perhaps the deepest ribbed horse in the world, his back ribs being tremendous but the deepness was carried on in the front with a great length of shoulder and forehand. Owing to his size there was a strong prejudice against him as a youngster. Lord Exeter was able to buy him for 180 pounds with a contingency of 500 pounds more if he won the Derby.

Stockwell won the Two Thousand Guineas and the St Leger by ten lengths, but failed in the Derby behind Daniel O'Rourke. He lost the Ascot Gold Cup by a head to Teddington, sire of the mare Marigold. It was out of Marigold that Stockwell produced Doncaster.

Stockwell had a beautiful golden coat, on which here and there were black spots, a feature of Stockwell descendants. Phar Lap had five spots on his off-side rear thigh, said to be in the shape of the Southern Cross. While not blessed with the best of tempers, during his stud career Stockwell sired the winners of 1150 races worth £358,989, as against £552,391 won by the progeny of St Simon.

NO DISCUSSION OF PHAR LAP'S FAMILY TREE is complete without comment from Dr W.J. Stewart McKay, who in 1933 wrote *The Evolution of
the Endurance, Speed and Staying Power of the Racehorse* and devoted an
entire chapter to the great horse. McKay wrote about Phar Lap with
the insight of an eyewitness, having spent many hours in the horse's
stall watching Tommy Woodcock fuss over the champion's feet and
legs. He regarded Phar Lap as 'the incarnation of Stockwell, you see
it in every line of his body'. His view of the significant influences of
the day on thoroughbred bloodlines gives an indication of how
Telford may have assessed the pedigree of Lot 41. McKay referred to
Stockwell as 'the Emperor of Stallions'.

Year after year Stockwell headed the winning sire list, and in 1866
his stock won 66,391 pounds, a sum that will take a lot of beating.

His sons won three Derbies, six St Legers, four Two Thousand
Guineas, and his daughters three One Thousand Guineas and one
Oaks. While Blair Athol was the greatest racer sired by Stockwell,
and was also successful at the stud, his line has taken a back seat and
the horse that handed on the virtues of his sire Stockwell was
Doncaster, the sire of the great Bend Or ...

Now that the St Simon sireline in England has declined, Bend Or
predominates, and his position as a sire and a founder of a line is
today greater than ever before. The deeds of Gallant Fox in America
have sent him to the head of affairs, and Night Raid, through
Nightmarch and Phar Lap and many other good horses, have kept
him in the limelight here in Australia. It is no exaggeration to say
that the Bend Or sire-line is the most successful in the world at
present.

McKay had Phar Lap measured as a four-year-old and then a year
later. In that period he had grown from 16.2¹/₄ hands to a little over 17

hands. His girth had expanded from 75¾ to 79 inches. Despite his regal stature, Phar Lap, according to McKay, was not without blemish.

> Phar Lap's head was just a plain head, nothing small or mean about it, but it lacked that beautiful moulding so characteristic of the thoroughbred ... his cheeks were large and flat, and the branches of his lower jaws were wide enough to fulfil the fist test with ease. His mouth was small, nostrils wide, and his muzzle small and refined.
>
> His neck was a little disappointing, as it lacked character and there was no sign of any crest ...
>
> Phar Lap's neck was not long, if anything it was a little short, but its strong muscles did not take away its flexibility. There was one great advantage in a neck like this in a big horse for it was not over-weighted, and one reason for it was that he had been gelded. There can be little doubt that the extra weight of the stallion's neck ... makes a tremendous difference to the condition of the racer's forelegs.

McKay did concede that Phar Lap had good points: 'When one looks at Phar Lap's hind-quarters one at once sees where his great strength lay: we could look at a thousand racers and never see anything so perfect as his croup, thigh, gaskins and cannons. His hind-quarters should have been modelled and cast as the "perfect hind-quarters".'

IF WE LOOK AT each of Phar Lap's grandparents we can see the influences of Stockwell, St Simon and Musket. Phar Lap was by Night Raid out of Entreaty. Night Raid's sire was Radium, a son of Bend Or who was a grandson of Stockwell. Radium was from Taia, which was by Donovan; Donovan won the Derby and the St Leger and was by the Derby winner Galopin, sire of St Simon. So the paternal grandsire of Phar Lap, Radium, had Stockwell and the sire of St Simon in his third ancestral generation.

Radium himself was a great stayer. Among other races he won the Doncaster Cup (over two miles and one furlong carrying 10.1), the Goodwood Cup and the Jockey Club Cup. Bend Or was twenty-five years old when he sired Radium. It was probably the best stayer he ever got. Radium was bred in 1903 and was one of the great field defeated by Spearmint in the Derby of 1906. He was a contemporary of two other noted stayers in The White Knight and Torpoint. He was only moderately successful as a sire, the best of his progeny being the Two Thousand Guineas winner Klessineas. Two sons of Radium were first-class racehorses in Australia, Rebus and King Offa. Rebus was an exceptionally good horse over any distance, winning the Sydney Cup, the Metropolitan with 9.10, the Epsom Handicap and the Villiers Stakes. At weight-for-age, however, Rebus was not in the class (but what horse was?) of Gloaming. King Offa won the Caulfield Cup in 1918.

The dam of Night Raid, Sentiment, was a granddaughter of Carbine (by Musket) and a great granddaughter of St Simon. Sentiment was by Spearmint (by Carbine), from Flair, who was a stablemate of Spearmint as a two- and three-year-old. After winning the Thousand Guineas in 1906, Flair was set for the Derby. Spearmint was to be prepared for the Grand Prix de Paris. When Flair went amiss, Spearmint's campaign was altered to include the Derby and he ultimately won both races. When their careers had finished the owners decided with a touch of romance that the pair should be mated. They produced Sentiment, the dam of Night Raid. Spearmint's great-grandfather on his dam side was the triple-crown winner Lord Lyon, another great horse by Stockwell.

Flair was by St Frusquin, a son of St Simon, out of Glare (by Ayrshire). Chiron, writing in *The Australasian* of 16 April 1932, commented:

> St Frusquin was a contemporary of Persimmon. They were two great horses and there was not more than a pound or two between them when they were racing as three-year-olds. Both were sons of St Simon and like Nightmarch and Phar Lap, two sons of Night Raid, they were of an exactly opposite type. St Frusquin was a brown horse of lovely quality, on short legs with a wonderful back and loins. He was perhaps a trifle short. Persimmon on the other hand was a lengthy bay, slightly on the leg, with the most perfect shoulders, budlike head and neck. Great quarters and straight hocks. St Frusquin won the Two Thousand Guineas but lost the Derby by a neck to Persimmon.

Glare's damline traced back to Stockwell in the fourth generation. Thus, Night Raid's dam had Musket, St Simon and Stockwell in her pedigree.

Phar Lap's dam, Entreaty, was a stoutly bred mare who broke down after her first race. Her sire, Winkie, the third of Phar Lap's 'grandparents', was by William the Third, a son of St Simon. William the Third's dam, Gravity, traced back to Stockwell in the second generation of her damline and in the fourth generation of the sire-line to Stockwell's brother, Rataplan. Winkie's dam, Conjure, was by Juggler II, a grandson of Lord Lyon (by Stockwell) and via the damline a great-grandson of Blair Athol (a Derby winner), also by Stockwell. Entreaty was from the mare Prayer Wheel, which was by Pilgrim's Progress out of Musket's granddaughter, Catherine Wheel.

Pilgrim's Progress was by Isonomy, from one of Stockwell's daughters, Isola Bella. Pilgrim's Progress was the sire of Abundance, winner of the AJC and Victoria Derbies and St Legers in 1902–03 and the Caulfield Stakes. Thus Phar Lap's fourth grandparent had Stockwell and Musket in her pedigree.

What do we learn from this? Perhaps Harry Telford was a genius because he plucked Phar Lap from a sales catalogue by his breeding and was able to have David Davis buy him for a song. Telford might also have just been lucky. When he was a strapper in the very early days of his short career as a jockey, he had the responsibility of caring for the fine stayer Prime Warden, who was out of a mare called Miss Kate. Miss Kate appears in Phar Lap's pedigree and was also the granddam of Blue Jacket, a leading New Zealand stayer. This obscure personal connection may have been the primary reason Telford chose Lot 41. History tells us that whatever the reason Telford was undoubtedly touched—perhaps for the only time in his life—by outrageous good fortune. Entreaty had twelve foals to race. Eight of them were by Night Raid. Only one of them was any good.

ONE SIDELIGHT TO the story of Phar Lap's breeding came in the week following the 1932 Agua Caliente Handicap. When Night Raid was exported from England, his equine companion was another entire named Cymric. And when, after seeing photographs of Phar Lap at Agua Caliente, the original trainer of Night Raid, Captain Tom Hogg, refused to believe that Nightmarch and Phar Lap were sired by the horse he knew as Night Raid. He contended that Cymric and Night Raid must have been maritime changelings, having been somehow confused in transit from England. This was despite the horse known in the Antipodes as Night Raid being described as 'the ugliest stallion in Australasia' and Nightmarch and Phar Lap being two very distinct types. Nightmarch was of a compact conformation, and was described by Chiron as being 'about as perfectly modelled as any horse we have ever seen in this country.'

Although a romantic notion, the story lacked credibility then, and still does so. Weatherbys, the long-time keepers of the Stud Book in England, produced certificates clearly describing each of the horses' markings as well as their breeding. It would have been impossible to have confused the two.

As we look forward, we can trace the blood of Phar Lap's family to some strong contemporary performers. Harry Telford did indeed know a stout pedigree when he saw one. But as a battling trainer, he needed to buy a racetrack performer, not a breeding influence. And, by a stroke of luck, he managed it.

Although Phar Lap's siblings were unremarkable racehorses, their contributions, particularly the mares, to breeding were significant. For example, the New Zealand mare Sunline, which has won the AJC Flight Stakes and Doncaster Handicap, the STC Coolmore Classic, plus two W.S. Cox Plates at Group One level, is a direct descendant through the damline of Fortune's Wheel, the first of Entreaty's foals by Night Raid. Sunline is thus a direct descendant of Phar Lap's older sister. In the same fashion, Research, which also won the AJC Flight Stakes, plus the AJC Oaks, the AJC Derby, the VRC Oaks, the STC Storm Queen Stakes, the VRC Wakeful Stakes and the AJC Furious Stakes, is a direct descendant through the damline of another of Phar Lap's sisters, Raphis, which was foaled in 1934.

As yet, no descendants of the family have won a Melbourne Cup. Monte Carlo, which did win the AJC and VRC Derbies, and the AJC St Leger, looked set to win the 1958 Cup, but was run down by Baystone in the shadows of the post. Monte Carlo was a grandson of Raphis.

Phar Lap's racing statistics

1. Race record

AT TWO YEARS (1929)

unpl–13 23.2.29 *RRC Nursery Handicap, first division (Rosehill; 5½ furlongs)* Exact (5–2 fav) 8.6 first; Cabaret Girl (10–1) 7.6 second; Pimento (3–1) 7.12 third. **Phar Lap H.C. Martin 6.11 last.** Margins: 2.5 lengths x 2 lengths. Time: 1:07.75.

unpl–16 2.3.29 *HRC Two-Year-Old Handicap (Hawkesbury; 5 furlongs)* Sheila (5–1) 7.10 first; Pure Tea (4–1) 8.0 second; Win Gold (8–1) 7.3 third. **Phar Lap F. Douglas 7.3 seventh.** Margins: 1.25 lengths x 2 lengths. Time: 1:04.0.

unpl–16 16.3.29 *RRC Nursery Handicap, first division (Rosehill; 6 furlongs)* My Talisman (5–1) 6.13 first; Peacemaker (2–1 fav) 8.3 second; Palmdale (20–1) 7.2 third. **Phar Lap H.C. Martin 8.2 not in first eight.** Margins: long head x long neck. Time: 1:15.25.

unpl–11 1.4.29 *AJC Easter Stakes (Randwick; 7 furlongs)* Carradale (9–4 eq fav) 8.2 first; Sir Ribble (14–1) 7.9 second; Pantheus (9–4 eq fav) 8.2 third. **Phar Lap J. Baker 7.6 eighth.** Margins: short head x 3 lengths. Time: 1:26.5.

1–21 27.4.29 *RRC Maiden Juvenile Handicap (Rosehill; 6 furlongs)* **Phar Lap (7–1) J. Baker 7.9 first;** Voleuse (4–1) 7.6 second; Pure Tea (5–2 fav) 8.12 third. Margins: 0.5 lengths x 1.5 length. Time: 1:15.5.

AT THREE YEARS (1929–30)

unpl–21 3.8.29 *AJC Denham Court Handicap (Warwick Farm; 6 furlongs)* Killarney (7–1) 8.13 first; Aussie (9–4 fav) 9.13 second; Shankara (6–1) 8.11 third. **Phar Lap J. Simpson 7.2 midfield.** Margins: 0.75 length x 0.75 length. Time: 1:13.0.

unpl–17 17.8.29 *RRC Three-Year-Old Handicap (Rosehill; 7 furlongs)* Firbolg (6–1) 8.10 and King Crow (9–2 eq fav) 8.7 dead heat first; Rostova (8–1) 7.12 third. **Phar Lap (8–1) J. Simpson 7.13 fourth.** Margins: dead heat x 1.5 lengths. Time: 1:27.75.

unpl–25 24.8.29 *RRC Three and Four-Year-Old Handicap (Rosehill; 7 furlongs)* Ticino (3–1 eq fav) 8.3 first; Violin Solo (10–1) 7.10 second; Woodgera (10–1) 7.11 third. **Phar Lap J. Brown 7.6 eighth.** Margins: 0.5 length x 2 lengths. Time: 1:27.0.

unpl–10 31.8.29 *AJC Warwick Stakes (Warwick Farm; 1 mile, WFA)* Limerick (5–1) 9.0 first; Mollison (4–7 fav) 8.11 second; Winalot (20–1) 9.3 third. **Phar Lap J. Brown 7.6 fourth.** Margins: 0.75 length x 1.75 lengths. Time: 1:38.75.

2–10 14.9.29 *Tattersall's Chelmsford Stakes (Randwick; 9 furlongs, WFA with penalties and allowances)* Mollison (2–1 eq fav) 9.4 first; **Phar Lap (10–1) J. Brown 7.6 second;** Winalot (2–1 eq fav) 9.11 third. Margins: 0.5 length x 3 lengths Time: 1:52.0.

1–12 21.9.29 *RRC Rosehill Guineas (Rosehill; 9 furlongs, set weights)* **Phar Lap (2–1 fav) J. Munro 8.5 first;** Lorason (8–1) 8.5 second; Holdfast (7–1) 8.5 third. Margins: 3 lengths x 2.5 lengths. Time: 1:52.0 (equal race record).

1–11 5.10.29 *AJC Derby (Randwick; 1½ miles, set weights)* **Phar Lap (5–4 fav) J. Pike 8.10 first;** Carradale (9–2) 8.10 second; Honour (9–2) 8.10 third. Margins: 3.5 lengths x 8 lengths. Time: 2: 31.25 (race record).

1–4 9.10.29 *AJC Craven Plate (Randwick; 1¼ miles, WFA)* **Phar Lap (5–4 eq fav) W. Duncan 7.8 first;** Mollison (5–4 eq fav) 8.11 second; Amounis (14–1) 9.1 third. Margins: 4 lengths x 10 lengths. Time: 2:11.25.

1–7 2.11.29 *VRC Victoria Derby (Flemington; 1½ miles, set weights)* **Phar Lap (2–9 fav) J. Pike 8.10 first;** Carradale (10–1) 8.10 second; Taisho (15–1) 8.10 third. Margins: 2 lengths x 0.5 length.Time: 2:31.25 (race record).

3–14 5.11.29 *VRC Melbourne Cup (Flemington; 2 miles, open handicap)* Nightmarch (6–1) 9.2 first; Paquito (33–1) 8.5 second; **Phar Lap (evens fav) R. Lewis 7.6 third.** Margins: 3 lengths x 1 length. Time: 3:26.5.

3–6 15.2.30 *VATC St George Stakes (Caulfield; 9 furlongs, WFA with penalties and allowances)* Amounis (6–4 fav) 9.8 first; Parsee (33–1) 9.2 second; **Phar Lap (7–4) R. Lewis 8.10 third.** Margins: 0.5 length x neck. Time: 1:53.75.

1–5 1.3.30 *VRC St Leger Stakes (Flemington; 1¾ miles, set weights)* **Phar Lap (1–2 fav) J. Pike 8.10 first;** Sir Ribble (4–1) 8.10 second; Lineage (5–1) 8.10 third. Margins: 5 lengths x 2 lengths. Time: 3: 01.25 (race record).

1–4 6.3.30 *VRC Governor's Plate (Flemington; 1½ miles, WFA)* **Phar Lap (4–9 fav) W. Elliott 7.13 first;** Lineage (33–1) 7.13 second; High Syce (5–2) 9.3 third. Margins: 4 lengths x 4 lengths. Time: 2:30.25 (race record).

1–5 8.3.30 *VRC King's Plate (Flemington; 2 miles, WFA)* **Phar Lap (1–10 fav) W. Elliott 7.11 first;** Second Wind (20–1) 8.11 second; Lineage (15–1) 7.11 third. Margins: 20 lengths x 3 lengths. Time: 3:25.0 (race record).

1–5 12.4.30 AJC *Chipping Norton Stakes (Warwick Farm; 1¹/₄ miles, WFA with penalties and allowances)* **Phar Lap (5–4 fav) J. Pike 8.10 first**; Amounis (2–1) 9.6 second; Nightmarch (5–2) 9.7 third. Margins: 2 lengths x neck. Time: 2:06.0.

1–3 19.4.30 AJC *St Leger (Randwick;1³/₄ miles, set weights)* **Phar Lap (1–20 fav) J. Pike 8.10 first**; Sir Ribble (20–1) 8.10 second; Peacemaker (20–1) 8.10 third. Margins: 3.5 lengths x 1.5 lengths. Time: 3: 07.0.

1–3 23.4.30 AJC *Cumberland Stakes (Randwick; 1³/₄ miles, WFA)* **Phar Lap W. Elliott 8.1 first**; Donald 9.0 second; Kidaides 9.0 third. No betting. Margins: 2 lengths x 20 lengths. Time: 2:58.75 (course record)

1–3 26.4.30 AJC *Plate (Randwick; 2¹/₄ miles, WFA)* **Phar Lap (2–5 fav) W. Elliott 7.13 first**; Nightmarch (9–4) 9.0 second; Donald (33–1) 9.1 third. Margins: 10 lengths x 0.75 length. Time: 3:49.5 (Australasian record).

1–2 10.5.30 SAJC *Elder Stakes (Morphettville; 9 furlongs, WFA)* **Phar Lap W. Elliott 8.4 first**; Fruition 8.13 second. Tote betting only; winner paid one pound, six shillings for one pound stake. Margin: 5 lengths. Time: 1:52.0.

1–6 17.5.30 SAJC *King's Cup (Morphettville; 1¹/₂ miles, quality handicap)* **Phar Lap J. Pike 9.5 first**; Kirrkie 7.10 and Nadean 8.2 dead heat second. Tote betting only; winner paid one pound, one shilling for one pound stake. Margins: 3.5 lengths x dead heat. Time: 2:34.0.

AT FOUR YEARS (1930–31)

2–10 30.8.30 AJC *Warwick Stakes (Warwick Farm; 1 mile, WFA with penalties and allowances)* Amounis (6–1) 9.0 first; **Phar Lap (10–9 fav) J. Pike 8.11 second**; Nightmarch (7–2) 9.3 third. Margins: short head x 3 lengths. Time: 1:38.0 (equalled track record).

1–7 13.9.30 *Tattersall's Chelmsford Stakes (Randwick; 9 furlongs, WFA with penalties and allowances)* **Phar Lap (1–5 fav) J. Pike 9.4 first**; Nightmarch (9–2) 9.11 second; Weotara (100–1) 7.6 third. Margins: 2.5 lengths x short neck. Time: 1:51.5.

1–7 20.9.30 RRC *Hill Stakes (Rosehill; 1 mile, WFA with penalties and allowances)* **Phar Lap (2–7 fav) J. Pike 9.4 first**; Nightmarch (4–1) 9.3 second; High Disdain (33–1) 9.2 third. Margins: 1 length x 1.5 lengths. Time: 1:40.0.

1–5 4.10.30 AJC *Spring Stakes (Randwick; 1¹/₂ miles, WFA)* **Phar Lap (1–10 fav) J. Pike 8.11 first**; Nightmarch (7–1) 9.5 second; Concentrate (33–1) 9.2 third. Margins: 0.5 length x 8 lengths. Time: 2:33.25.

1–4 8.10.30 AJC *Craven Plate (Randwick; 1¹/₄ miles, WFA)* **Phar Lap (1–6 fav) J. Pike 8.11 first**; Nightmarch (5–1) 9.4 second; Donald (20–1) 9.2 third. Margins: 6 lengths x 10 lengths. Time: 2:03.0 (Australasian record).

1–3 11.10.30 AJC *Randwick Plate (Randwick; 2 miles, WFA)* **Phar Lap J. Pike 8.11 first**; Donald 9.2 second; Concentrate 9.2 third. No straight-out betting. Margins: 2 lengths x 3 lengths. Time: 3: 36.25.

1–6 25.10.30 MVRC *WS Cox Plate (Moonee Valley; 9½ furlongs, WFA)* **Phar Lap (1–7 fav) J. Pike 8.11 first**; Tregilla (10–1) 7.11 second; Mollison (10–1) 9.1 third. Margins: 4 lengths x 1 length. Time: 1:59.25.

1–5 1.11.30 VRC *Melbourne Stakes (Flemington; 1¼ miles, WFA)* **Phar Lap (1–5 fav) J. Pike 8.11 first**; Tregilla (16–1) 7.12 second; Amounis (6–1) 9.0 third. Margins: 3 lengths x 4 lengths. Time: 2: 04.5.

1–15 4.11.30 VRC *Melbourne Cup (Flemington; 2 miles, open handicap)* **Phar Lap (8–11 fav) J. Pike 9.12 first**; Second Wind (50–1) 8.12 second; Shadow King (50–1) 8.4 third. Margins: 3 lengths x 0.75 length. Time: 3:27.75.

1–5 6.11.30 VRC *Linlithgow Stakes (Flemington; 1 mile, WFA)* **Phar Lap (1–7 fav) J. Pike 8.11 first**; Mollison (33–1) 8.13 second; Mystic Peak (33–1) 9.2 third. Margins: 4 lengths x neck. Time: 1:37.0.

1–3 8.11.30 VRC *CB Fisher Plate (Flemington; 1½ miles, WFA)* **Phar Lap J. Pike 8.11 first**; Second Wind 9.1 second; Lineage 8.9 third. No betting. Margins: 3.5 lengths x 4 lengths. Time: 2:48.25.

1–4 14.2.31 VATC *St George Stakes (Caulfield; 9 furlongs, WFA with penalties)* **Phar Lap (1–14 fav) J. Pike 9.4 first**; Induna 8.5 second; Glare 8.13 third. Margins: 2.5 lengths x 2.25 lengths. Time: 1:54.75.

1–10 21.2.31 VATC *Futurity Stakes (Caulfield; 7 furlongs, WFA with penalties and allowances)* **Phar Lap (1–2 fav) J. Pike 10.3 first**; Mystic Peak (33–1) 10.2 second; Taurus (100–1) 8.11 third. Margins: neck x 1 length. Time: 1:27.25.

1–4 28.2.31 VRC *Essendon Stakes (Flemington; 1¼ miles, WFA with penalties and allowances)* **Phar Lap J. Pike 9.7 first**; Lambra 8.0 second; Mira Donna 7.7 third. No Betting. Margins: 3 lengths x 4 lengths. Time: 2:05.25.

1–5 4.3.31 VRC *King's Plate (Flemington; 1½ miles, WFA with penalties and allowances)* **Phar Lap J. Pike 9.7 first**; Glare 8.0 second; El Rey 8.3 third. No betting. Margins: 1.25 lengths x 1.5 lengths. Time: 2:37.25.

2–4 7.3.31 VRC *CM Lloyd Stakes (Flemington; 1 mile, WFA with penalties and allowances)* Waterline (7–2) 8.0 first; **Phar Lap (1–3 fav) J. Pike 9.7 second**; Temoin (33–1) 8.0 third. Margins: neck x 3 lengths. Time: 1:38.0.

AT FIVE YEARS (1931–32)

1–6 25.8.31 *WRC Underwood Stakes (Williamstown; 1 mile, WFA)* **Phar Lap (2–1 fav) W. Elliott 9.0 first**; Rondalina (33–1) 7.6 second; Wise Force (9–4) 9.3 third. Margins: 1.75 lengths x neck. Time: 1:42.5.

1–6 5.9.31 *VATC Memsie Stakes (Caulfield; 9 furlongs, WFA with penalties)* **Phar Lap (1–6 fav) J. Pike 9.8 first**; Rondalina (20–1) 6.11 second; Waterline (15–1) 9.8 third. Margins: 3.5 lengths x head. Time: 1:52.75.

1–4 19.9.31 *RRC Hill Stakes (Rosehill; 1 mile, WFA with penalties and allowances)* **Phar Lap J. Pike 9.0 first**; Chide 9.0 second; Waugoola 9.0 third. No betting. Margins: 1.5 lengths x 3 lengths. Time: 1:39.5.

1–7 3.10.31 *AJC Spring Stakes (Randwick; 1½ miles, WFA)* **Phar Lap J. Pike 9.2 first**; Chide 9.3 second; The Dimmer 9.3 third. No betting. Margins: 1.25 lengths x 3 lengths. Time: 2:33.75.

1–4 7.10.31 *AJC Craven Plate (Randwick; 1¼ miles, WFA)* **Phar Lap J. Pike 9.1 first**; Pentheus 9.4 second; Chide 9.1 third. No betting. Margins: 4 lengths x 3.5 lengths. Time: 2:02.5 (Australian record).

1–2 10.10.31 *AJC Randwick Plate (Randwick; 2 miles, WFA)* **Phar Lap J. Pike 9.3 first**; Chide 9.4 second. No betting. Margin: 4 lengths. Time: 3:31.0.

1–7 24.10.31 *MVRC WS Cox Plate (Moonee Valley; 9½ furlongs, WFA)* **Phar Lap (1–14 fav) J. Pike 9.4 first**; Chatham 7.11 second; Johnnie Jason 7.11 third. Margins: 2.5 lengths x 2 lengths. Time: 2:01.5.

1–4 31.10.31 *VRC Melbourne Stakes (Flemington; 1¼ miles, WFA)* **Phar Lap J. Pike 9.1 first**; Concentrate 9.1 second; Veilmond 9.0 third. No betting. Margins: 0.5 length x 1.25 lengths. Time: 2:06.5.

unpl–14 3.11.31 *VRC Melbourne Cup (Flemington; 2 miles, open handicap)* White Nose (8–1) 6.12 first; Shadow King (25–1) 8.7 second; Concentrate (4–1) 8.10 third. **Phar Lap (3 fav) J. Pike 10.10 eighth**. Margins: 2 length x neck. Time: 3:26.0.

1–11 20.3.32 *Agua Caliente Handicap (Tijuana, Mexico; 1¼ miles, set weights)* **Phar Lap (6–5 fav) W. Elliott 9.3 first**; Reveille Boy (3–1) 8.6 second; Scimitar (15–1) 7.2 third. Margins: 2 lengths x 1 length. Time: 2:02.8 (track record).

2. Race record summary

IN AUSTRALIA

Age	Starts	Wins	Seconds	Thirds	Unplaced	Prize money (£Aus)
Two	5	1	–	–	4	182
Three	20	13	1	2	4	26,794
Four	16	14	2	–	–	24,871
Five	9	8	–	–	1	4,578
Total	50	36	3	2	9	56,425

IN NORTH AMERICA

Age	Starts	Wins	Seconds	Thirds	Unplaced	Prize money ($US)
Five	1	1	–	–	–	50,050

Note: The prize money from the Agua Caliente was converted by Australian racing officials, for the purpose of recording Phar Lap's total stakes winnings, to £10,298. In *Phar Lap*, Isabel Carter argues that the correct conversion, based on the exchange rates of the time, should have been £12,843 (although she suggests that the 'official' converted figure was £10,313). Elsewhere, the conversion has been put as high as £13,700. Thus, different sources quote different figures for Phar Lap's total career earnings.

Based on the official conversion of the Agua Caliente stakes (to £10,298) Phar Lap's career winnings in Australian pounds are £66,723.

3. Prize money

IN AUSTRALIA

AT TWO YEARS

Date	Race	Finished	Stakes*
23.2.29	RRC Nursery Handicap	unplaced	–
2.3.29	HRC Two-Year-Old Handicap	unplaced	–
16.3.29	RRC Nursery Handicap	unplaced	–
1.4.29	AJC Easter Stakes	unplaced	–
27.4.29	RRC Maiden Juvenile Handicap	first	182

AT THREE YEARS

Date	Race	Finished	Stakes*
3.8.29	AJC Denham Court Handicap	unplaced	–
17.8.29	RRC Three-Year-Old Handicap	unplaced	–
24.8.29	RRC Three and Four-Year-Old Handicap	unplaced	–
31.8.29	AJC Warwick Stakes	unplaced	–
14.9.29	Tattersall's Chelmsford Stakes	second	200
21.9.29	RRC Rosehill Guineas	first	913
5.10.29	AJC Derby	first	7135
9.10.29	AJC Craven Plate	first	2205
2.11.29	VRC Victoria Derby	first	4456
5.11.29	VRC Melbourne Cup	third	1000
15.2.30	VATC St George Stakes	third	75
1.3.30	VRC St Leger Stakes	first	1691
6.3.30	VRC Governor's Plate	first	749
8.3.30	VRC King's Plate	first	1112
12.4.30	AJC Chipping Norton Stakes	first	747
19.4.30	AJC St Leger	first	2478
23.4.30	AJC Cumberland Stakes	first	1457
26.4.30	AJC Plate	first	1451
10.5.30	SAJC Elder Stakes	first	325
17.5.30	SAJC King's Cup	first	800

* All stakes in Australian pounds

AT FOUR YEARS

Date	Race	Finished	Stakes*
30.8.30	AJC Warwick Stakes	second	200
13.9.30	Tattersall's Chelmsford Stakes	first	1033
20.9.30	RRC Hill Stakes	first	597
4.10.30	AJC Spring Stakes	first	1467
8.10.30	AJC Craven Plate	first	1830
11.10.30	AJC Plate	first	1465
25.10.30	MVRC WS Cox Plate	first	850
1.11.30	VRC Melbourne Stakes	first	1000
4.11.30	VRC Melbourne Cup	first	9429
6.11.30	VRC Linlithgow Stakes	first	1000
8.11.30	VRC CB Fisher Plate	first	1000
14.2.31	VATC St George Stakes	first	600
21.2.31	VATC Futurity Stakes	first	2600
28.2.31	VRC Essendon Stakes	first	700
4.3.31	VRC King's Plate	first	700
7.3.31	VRC CM Lloyd Stakes	second	200

AT FIVE YEARS

Date	Race	Finished	Stakes*
25.8.31	WRC Underwood Stakes	first	350
5.9.31	VATC Memsie Stakes	first	500
19.9.31	RRC Hill Stakes	first	444
3.10.31	AJC Spring Stakes	first	779
7.10.31	AJC Craven Plate	first	940
10.10.31	AJC Plate	first	740
24.10.31	MVRC WS Cox Plate	first	500
31.10.31	VRC Melbourne Stakes	first	525
3.11.31	VRC Melbourne Cup	unplaced	–

* All stakes in Australian pounds

IN NORTH AMERICA

Date	Race	Finished	Stakes**
20.3.32	Agua Caliente Handicap	first	50,050

** Stakes in US dollars. Some reports record this stakes figure as $50,000.

4. Jockeys

Course	Starts	Wins	Seconds	Thirds	Unplaced
Jim Pike	30	27	2	–	1
Billy Elliott	7	7	–	–	–
Jack Brown	3	–	1	–	2
Jack Baker	2	1	–	–	1
Bobby Lewis	2	–	–	2	–
H.C. 'Cash' Martin	2	–	–	–	2
Jim Simpson	2	–	–	–	2
Billy Duncan	1	1	–	–	–
Jim Munro	1	1	–	–	–
Frank Douglas	1	–	–	–	1

5. Racetracks

Course	Starts	Wins	Seconds	Thirds	Unplaced	Success Rate
Moonee Valley	2	2	–	–	–	100.00%
Morphettville	2	2	–	–	–	100.00%
Agua Caliente	1	1	–	–	–	100.00%
Williamstown	1	1	–	–	–	100.00%
Randwick	14	12	1	–	1	85.71%
Flemington	14	11	1	1	1	78.57%
Caulfield	4	3	–	1	–	75.00%
Rosehill	8	4	–	–	4	50.00%
Warwick Farm	4	1	1	–	2	25.00%
Hawkesbury	1	–	–	–	1	0.00%

Glossary

apprentice: Jockeys learn to become jockeys by serving an apprenticeship to a trainer. Driven by a love for horses or a distaste for formal education, children of small stature leave school as soon as they are able and join a trainer's stable where they perform strappers' tasks while developing their riding skills. Trainers are responsible for supervising the apprentice's development in all aspects of racing. Traditionally, the ability to frequently and subserviently say 'Sir' was considered evidence of the success of the trainer's tutelage. In the past, potential jockeys could begin their apprenticeship on their fourteenth birthday and remained apprenticed to trainers until the age of twenty-one.

at the distance: Historically, racecourses have had a marker 240 yards from the finish. This marker is 'The Distance'.

backmarkers: Horses that race at the rear of the field as part of their race tactics.

betting ring: The fraternity of bookmakers taking bets on course on race day. Within the fraternity, the most senior are the rails bookmakers— and they have the 'biggest books' or, to put it more accurately, the deepest bags. The ring conjures images of uncompromising confrontation and when a leviathan punter steps in occasionally one or more bookies will 'take him on'.

birdcage: The enclosure where, in the past, horses on raceday were stabled at the course. Only authorised people were admitted: punters tended to line up against the fence of the Birdcage and peer at the horses.

bloodlines: A horse's pedigree.

bookmaker: A person who sets a market for a race and takes bets on it. The skill of bookmaking is to take as few bets as possible on the horse that wins the race and as many bets as possible on those that don't.

bog track: Depending on the weather in the lead-up to the races, the track could be anything from very dry to extremely wet. The graduations used in Australia to describe track conditions are fast (as in perfect or close to perfect), good, dead, slow and heavy (as in very wet underhoof). On extremely wet days, you could hear talk of a bog track.

certainty beaten: A horse that would have won for sure, but for suffering interference, being poorly ridden, or finding some other unlikely or unfair way to lose.

claim/claiming [seven]: In certain races, an apprentice jockey is given an allowance or claim to compensate for his lack of experience. Thus, in pre-metric days, an apprentice could claim up to 7 lb off the horse's allotted weight; today the maximum claim is 3 kg. As the apprentice wins more races, the allowance is reduced. Eventually the apprentice becomes such a good rider that punters even back his mounts.

climb: When a horse tires at the end of a race, it sometimes seems to lift the front legs higher than usual and thus shorten stride. This is described as 'climbing', as though the horse is trying to climb stairs.

clocker: A regular at trackwork with the rare ability to recognise horses without jockey's colours—in the darkness or the early-morning mist, or both—from the other side of the racecourse, which gives them the ability to time a horse's training performance. The results of a clocker's observations are always accurate and are expressed as, for example, 'Three furlongs in thirty-six.' This ability is developed over a lifetime of pre-dawn attendances. A good clocker truly is a great judge of a horse.

colt: A horse less than four years of age which has not been gelded. Once a colt becomes a four-year-old (on 1 August for thoroughbred horses in the southern hemisphere) it is called a horse. Once it assumes stud duties, it is a stallion.

compound: An unfit horse, or one that has run too quickly early in a race or has fought with its jockey, will tire or 'compound' in the straight.

connections: The owners and the trainer of a horse.

crack: In equine circles, the very best—be this horse or jockey. Thus Banjo Paterson, in describing the search for the last son of Old Regret, told how 'all the cracks had gathered to the fray'.

Cup: Although there are many cups won in racing, there is only one Cup: the Melbourne Cup. Now run on the first Tuesday in November, it was first run in 1861. Over two miles (now 3200 metres) it is a Handicap race for all comers.

Derby: The classic 'Classic' race of the turf, traditionally run over a mile and a half and restricted to three-year-olds. Like many of racing's traditions it was imported from England, where the first Derby was run at Epsom Downs in Surrey in 1780. The first Derby was won by Diomed, owned by Sir Charles Bunbury, who was a steward of the Jockey Club in England. The race was named after the winner of the toss of a coin held between Bunbury and the 12th Earl of Derby. The Oaks is the female equivalent of the Derby, restricted to three-year-old fillies, first run in 1779 and named after the Earl of Derby's Surrey residence.

desperate: A gambler who bets for the betting and not for the money.

drench: A dose of liquid medication given to a horse, often forcefully to ensure it is completely swallowed.

entire: A horse which has not been gelded.

favourite: The horse the betting ring determines as having the best chance of winning, and thus starts at the shortest price. If two or more contenders start at the same shortest price, they are said to be equal favourites.

filly: The female equivalent of a colt. Once a filly reaches its fourth birthday it becomes a mare. Once a mare gets to stud she becomes a broodmare.

first-up: A horse resuming from a spell is said to be 'first-up'. Thus a win by a horse in its first race after a spell is a first-up victory. Few horses are fully fit at their first run from a break, so first-up victories are relatively rare. Phar Lap, for example, didn't win first-up until the autumn of 1931.

foot: An Imperial measure of length, equalling 12 inches or 30.48 centimetres. As a foot is a unit of measure, logically its plural should be foots, but as it derives from the anatomical foot, the plural of the unit was often referred to as feet. Occasionally, in the spirit of compromise, the plural was expressed in the singular (as in 'five foot tall').

furlong: One eighth of a mile. The Imperial mile is 1760 yards, so a furlong is 220 yards. When racecourses began to use metric measures (on 1 August 1972 in Australia), a furlong was approximated to 200 metres (in fact it is 201.168 metres). This approximation has caused heartburn for timekeepers and traditionalists. The 2-mile handicap that was the Melbourne Cup is now run over 3200 metres—18.688 metres short of its traditional journey. Records for all events are therefore either 'metric' or 'Imperial', making comparisons between eras even more difficult.

gelding: A male horse which has had its testicles surgically removed. As a rule, geldings tend to be easier to train.

get a price: To back a horse at good odds relative to the odds generally on offer for that horse.

get out: When a punter 'gets out', he or she ends his or her betting for the day with at least no more than a small loss despite having at one point been losing heavily.

guinea: A guinea was a British gold coin of the value of 21 shillings. The coin was taken from circulation in 1813, but the term was retained (still meaning 21 shillings) and was regularly used to price the sale of horses.

handicap: A race in which entrants are given advantages or disadvantages in weight, based upon their age, sex, potential and previous performances, in order to equalise their chances of winning. Good horses get the most weight. Great horses are so severely handicapped that they usually concentrate on weight for age, other set weight events or, if entires or mares, get sent to stud.

handicapper: The race-club employee given the task of allotting weights to all entrants in handicap events. The handicapper's ambition is, as far as possible, to give every entrant an equal chance of winning. For major handicaps such as the Melbourne Cup, the handicapper is obliged to announce the weights weeks, sometimes months, before raceday. For 'classic' races such as Derbies and Oaks, and also in weight-for-age events, the handicapper plays no part, as all entries receive set weights.

hands: A horse's height is measured in hands, one hand equalling 4 inches (11.6 centimetres). The height is the vertical distance from the middle of the horse's withers (the lumpy bit where the neck joins the back) to the ground. Generally, a horse is greater than 14.2 hands (58 inches) tall. A diminutive horse is sometimes called a pony, although this distinction is more correctly made on the basis of breed. Most thoroughbreds are between 15 and 17 hands tall.

hang: Suggested as appropriate for some jockeys (see 'shout through your pocket') but more generally refers to the tendency for a tired horse to deviate from a straight line.

horseman: Someone—trainer, jockey or strapper—unusually gifted in the management of horses. To be described as a horseman is to receive one of life's rare universal compliments; it is deserved by very few.

jockey: The man, woman, boy or girl in the saddle. The ability of a jockey can be vital and involves much more than just steering. Good jockeys are usually seen on the best horses in the big races; unsuccessful jockeys are unsuccessful for a reason. All jockeys are relatively short, some positively pint-sized and most are astonishingly brave.

leaders of the ring: The most respected (and thus the richest) bookmakers.

length: Winning margins and the margins between place-getters are measured in lengths. A length is the distance from the winning horse's nose to the end of its hindquarters. As it is defined in terms of the size of the winning horse, a length is a variable measure, although in reality the variation in the length of a length is relatively small. On average, a length is slightly greater than 2 metres. Margins of less than a length are either fractions of a length, or a neck, a half-neck, a head or a half-head. Lesser margins (a short half-head and a nose) were not introduced until the advent of the photo finish.

line of betting: A favourite (or equal favourites) is said to be on the first line of betting. The horse or horses with the next lowest odds are in the 'second line' of betting.

maiden: A race restricted to horses that are yet to win a race.

mile: A mile is 1760 yards, 8 furlongs, or 1609 metres.

odds: The probability of a particular horse winning a race. Initially set by the bookmaker, odds change in response to the amount of money bet on each horse in the field. As money goes on a horse (the horse is backed) the odds are reduced: according to the market (the punters and their money), the probability of the horse winning has increased. For example, odds of 3–1 means the market gives the horse a 25 per cent chance of winning (one chance in four). A bet of £100 at 3–1 may be quoted £300 to £100: if successful, the punter will receive £300 plus the original stake of £100.

odds-on: As a horse is backed its odds shorten. If the weight of money, or plunge, is great enough, the horse will go from odds-against to odds-on (that is, the bookie will give the horse a greater than 50 per cent chance of winning).

pound (£): A monetary unit in Australia, New Zealand and the UK during the Phar Lap era. There were 20 shillings in a pound and 12 pennies in a shilling.

pound (lb): A measure of weight. An avoirdupois pound is divided into 16 ounces. A pound is equivalent to 0.454 kg; 1 kg is equivalent to 2.203 lb.

quid: A colloquial term for the monetary pound. A quick quid is money earned with little effort, usually by dishonest means. Many a quick quid has been won on the racetrack.

saddle: The lightweight leather seat upon which a jockey sits when riding. In fact, in race riding the saddle is as small as possible, to reduce its weight, and is really only a device for connecting the stirrups, upon which the jockey crouches, to the horse. The saddle is part of the total allotted weight that the horse must carry. Thus, when jockeys are struggling to get down to a horse's allocation they are keen to have as light a saddle as possible. If the jockey is light and requires extra to make up the designated weight, thin pieces of lead are added to bags under the saddle.

salute: When a horse wins it is said to salute the judge. Even today, when the place-getters return to scale, they are met by stewards at the winner's stall and desultory salutes are exchanged between the jockeys and the chief steward.

save: Having backed the Amounis/Phar Lap combination in the Caulfield and Melbourne Cups doubles on the assumption that Phar Lap would be reserved for the latter race, big punter Eric Connolly backed Phar Lap to win both Cups as insurance in case Phar Lap ended up running at Caulfield. In doing so, he was said to be 'saving' on Phar Lap.

shift out: A horse that moves away from the fence, usually to get a clear run or to find a firmer and thus faster part of the track, is said to 'shift out'. Alternatively, a horse may also shift in towards the fence, usually when put under pressure.

short price: When betting on a horse, if the odds are low (probability is high), the price is 'short'.

shout through your pocket: A horse is a favourite because most of the money is on it. When a favourite is beaten, the majority of punters are disgruntled, and try to retrieve their gruntle by abusing the jockey, as it is always the jockey's fault when a favourite doesn't win. The abuse the jockey receives as he returns to scale is the punters 'shouting through their pockets'.

sixpence: A silver coin worth six pennies.

spell: A break from racing and training. Invariably a horse being spelled is turned out into a paddock to allow it to rest, to put on weight and, in the case of younger horses, to grow.

stable: Horses are housed in a physical structure called 'stables'. The horses under the care of a particular trainer are collectively called his 'stable'.

stakes: The prize money on offer in a race. Events offering large bounties for the winner and place-getters are often called 'Stakes' races (as in the Futurity Stakes).

starting price (SP) bookmaker: An illegal, off-course bookmaker who traditionally accepted bets in pubs or over the telephone. Such a bookie did not quote odds, but relied on the odds being offered at the track when the race began to determine the extent of his or her payout.

stayer: A horse competitive in races run over distances at and beyond 2000 metres (a mile and a quarter). It is not just a question of being able to run that distance—after all, just about every horse can run 2 miles, but some take longer to complete the course than others. Only the good stayers can do so at the speed needed to win. In contrast, a sprinter is a horse that races over shorter distances, from 800 to 1400 metres (4 to 7 furlongs). A miler, not surprisingly, is at its best at or around 1600 metres (1 mile).

stone: A measure of weight equivalent to 14 lb or 6.356 kg. Until 1972, weight as carried by horses was expressed in stones and pounds, and can be in one of a number of notations: 9 stone 7 pounds; 9 stone 7; 9.7 (the form used throughout this book); or 9 st 7 lb (9 stone 7 is 133 lb or 60.382 kg).

straight-out bet: To bet for a win only. When there is a short-priced favourite or the field is small, bookies will take only win bets. A horse needs to totally dominate a race, as Phar Lap often did, before they won't bet at all.

strapper: A strapper is a stablehand with the specific task of caring for a horse. Strappers are usually allocated a number of horses at any particular time.

street smarts: Instinctive survival cunning developed in a harsh environment, and there have been few environments tougher than the racetracks and back streets of the Great Depression.

totalisator: Also called the tote. Rather than offering fluctuating odds as bookies do, the tote is a machine that offers successful punters an equal division of the total betting pool for a race, minus a set percentage. In other words, the tote gathers all the money invested, takes out its share and splits the rest equally between those who've backed the winner. The TAB, as we know it today, is a much, much bigger totalisator animal than the tote operations of the 1930s.

trainer: A person who prepares horses for their racetrack engagements. A good trainer is one capable of getting the most out of his stable—a fact which not all punters realise. A 'top' trainer usually has a stable full of beautifully bred horses and mixes with the richest of company. A 'battling' trainer has to make do with loyal or unsuccessful owners and unfashionably bred horses. As Harry Telford and many others have proved, battling trainers can succeed, at least for a while.

waste: Jockeys often struggle to get their weight low enough to be able to ride a horse at its allocated handicap. Jim Pike struggled with his weight throughout his career. Starvation, exercise and sweating are the methods used to reduce weight and these are collectively called 'wasting'.

weight-for-age (WFA): A method of weight allocation for horses that makes allowances for the age and sex of the horse and the time of the racing season. This means horses of different ages and either gender can compete in the same race under the most equal of conditions. The very best races are run under the weight-for-age scale, as it is said to allow the best horse to win. The scale has its origins in Great Britain in the eighteenth century, was revised by the English Jockey Club handicapper, Admiral Rous, in 1855 and has been modified fractionally a few times since.

welter: An often poor standard open-class handicap, where every horse in the field is given a relatively heavy weight.

work: A horse in training is a horse in work.

yard: An Imperial measurement, a yard is 3 feet, or 0.9144 metres. There are 12 inches in a foot (36 inches in a yard).

yearlings: One-year-old horses. In Australia, every horse increases in age by one year on 1 August, regardless of when it was born. This is to standardise horses' ages, a useful tool for judging eligibility for entry to races restricted to horses of a particular age (such as the Derby, which is limited to three-year-olds). Breeders wishing to have precocious two-year-old racers try to have the horse born on or as soon after 1 August as possible. Premature births can be embarrassing, so it is thought that stud-owners tend not to walk the breeding paddocks in the last few days of July.

Further reading

BOOKS

Bill Ahern, *A Century of Winners: The Saga of 121 Melbourne Cups*; Boolarong Publications, Brisbane, 1982

Tony Arrold, *Champions*; Tralca Publications, Sydney, 1980

Tony Arrold, *More Champions*; Tralca Publications, Sydney, 1983

D.L. Bernstein, *First Tuesday in November: The Story of the Melbourne Cup*; William Heinemann Limited, Melbourne, 1969

Ross du Bourg, *The Australian and New Zealand Thoroughbred (3rd Ed)*; Penguin Books, Melbourne, 1991

Scobie Breasley and Christopher Poole, *Scobie, A Lifetime in Racing*; Queen Anne Press, London, 1984

Isabel Carter, *Phar Lap, The story of the big horse*; Lansdowne Press, Melbourne, 1964

Maurice Cavanough and Meurig Davies, *Cup Day: The Story of the Melbourne Cup, 1861–1960*; FW Cheshire, Melbourne, 1960

Maurice Cavanough, *The Caulfield Cup*; Jack Pollard Pty Limited, Sydney, 1976

Marc Fiddian, *The Victoria Derby*; Pakenham Gazette, Pakenham, 1991

David Hickie, *Gentlemen of the Australian Turf*; Angus & Robertson, Sydney, 1986

John Hislop, *Breeding For Racing*; Martin Secker & Warburg Ltd, London, 1976

Warwick Hobson, *Racing's All-Time Greats*; Thoroughbred Press-Horwitz Grahame Books Pty Ltd, Sydney, 1986

Bert Lillye, *Backstage of Racing*; John Fairfax Marketing, Sydney, 1985

WJ Stewart McKay, *The Evolution of the Endurance, Speed and Staying Power of the Racehorse*; Hutchinson & Co. Publishers Limited, London, 1933

Neil Marks, *Tales for all Seasons*; HarperSports, Sydney, 1997

Miller's Guide 1999 Edition; Miller Form, Melbourne, 1999

Roger Mortimer and Peter Willett, *Great Racehorses of the World*; Michael Joseph, London, 1969

Roger Mortimer and Peter Willett, *More Great Racehorses of the World*; Michael Joseph, London, 1972

John O'Hara, *A Mug's Game: A History of Gaming and Betting in Australia*

John Pacini, *A Century Galloped By: The First 100 Years of the Victoria Racing Club*; Victoria Racing Club, Melbourne, 1988

Martin Painter and Richard Waterhouse, *The Principal Club: A History of the Australian Jockey Club*; Allen & Unwin, Sydney, 1992

Neville Penton, *A Racing Heart: The Story of the Australian Turf*; William Collins Pty Ltd, Sydney, 1987

Arn Rogers and Warwick Hobson, *$100,000 Winner's Circle*; Turf Monthly Pty Limited, Sydney, 1973

Jack Spinty, *Phar Lap: World's Greatest Racehorse*; first published by the author in Sydney in 1932

Richard Waterhouse, *Private Pleasure, Public Leisure: A History of Australian Popular Culture Since 1788*

B.M. Wicks, *The Racehorse, An Introduction to Thoroughbred Breeding*; Libra Books, Hobart, 1990

Michael Wilkinson, *The Phar Lap Story*; Schwartz Publishing Group, Melbourne, 1980

Jan Wositsky, *Tommy Woodcock 1905–1985*; Greenhouse Publications, Melbourne, 1986

NEWSPAPERS, PERIODICALS AND MAGAZINES

The Advertiser (Adelaide), *The Age* (Melbourne), *The Argus* (Melbourne), *The Arrow* (Sydney), *The Australasian* (Melbourne), *The Bloodstock Breeders' Review* (London), *Daily Pictorial* (Sydney), *Daily Telegraph* (Sydney), *The Evening News* (Sydney), *The Herald* (Melbourne), *Labor Daily* (Sydney), *Listener In* (Melbourne), *The New York Times* (New York), *Racetrack* (Sydney), *The Referee* (Sydney), *San Francisco Chronicle* (San Francisco), *Smith's Weekly* (Sydney), *The Sport* (Adelaide), *The Sporting Globe* (Melbourne), *The Sporting Judge* (Melbourne), *The Sun* (Sydney), *The Sun News-Pictorial* (Melbourne), *The Sunday News* (Sydney), *The Sunday Telegraph* (Sydney), *Sydney Mail* (Sydney), *The Sydney Morning Herald* (Sydney), *The Sydney Sportsman* (Sydney), *Truth* (Melbourne), *Truth* (Sydney), *Turf Monthly* (Sydney).

Sources

Chapter 1
PAGE NO.
7 Jim Marsh: interview with the authors, January 2000

He could be anything.
9 *The Bloodstock Breeders Review*, London, 1929
10–11 Harry Telford: *The Herald* (Melbourne), 5.11.30, p.7
12 Tommy Woodcock: Jan Wositzky, *Tommy Woodcock 1905–1985*; Greenhouse Publications, Melbourne 1986, p.24

Chapter 2
14–15 C.J. Graves: *The Referee*, 13.4.1932 p.3
16 A.B. Gray: *The Referee*, 13.4.1932 p.3
20–1 *The Sunday News*: 28.4.1929, p.2
22 Tommy Woodcock: Jan Wositzky, *Tommy Woodcock 1905–1985*; Greenhouse Publications, Melbourne 1986, p.25

Chapter 3
25 CJ Graves: *The Referee*, 13.4.1932 p.1
26 *Truth*: 1.9.1929, p.2
26 Jim Pike: *Daily Telegraph*, 26.3.1936, p.31
26–7 Bill Cook: quoted by John Bartle, 'The Day They Buried the Big Horse'; *Turf Monthly*, April, 1982, p.9
27 *Truth*: 22.9.1929, p.2
28 Snowden: *The Australasian*, 12.10.1929, p.20
30–1 AB Gray, *The Referee*, 13.4.1932 p.3
31–2 Peter Lawson: interview with Bill Casey, *The Sun*, 9.8.1983, p.15
34 Jim Pike: *Daily Telegraph*, 21.4.1936, p.23
35 Panacre: *The Arrow* 1.11.1929, p.1
37 Jim Pike: *Sunday Pictorial*, 3.11.1929, p.2
39 *Sydney Morning Herald*: 6.11.1929, p.17
39 Bobby Lewis: *Daily Telegraph-Pictorial*, 6.11.29, p.2
39 Tommy Woodcock: Jan Wositzky, *Tommy Woodcock 1905–1985*; Greenhouse Publications, Melbourne 1986, p.28

40 Jim Marsh: interview with the authors, January 2000
40 W.J. Stewart McKay: *The Referee*, 22.1.1930, p.7
44 *Truth*: 1.12.1929, p.2

Chapter 4
46 Tommy Woodcock: Jan Wositzky, *Tommy Woodcock 1905–1985*; Greenhouse Publications, Melbourne 1986, p.30
46 Jim Pike: *Daily Telegraph*, 9.4.1936, p.35
48 Musket: *The Sydney Mail*, 16.4.1930, p.50
50 Chiron: *The Australasian*, 3.5.1930, p.20
50 Vedette: *The Referee*, 30.4.1930, p.1
51 Jim Pike: *The Referee*, 28.5.1930, p.2
52 Jim Marsh: interview with the authors, January 2000
52 A. McAulay: *The Referee*, 28.5.1930, p.5
54 *The Advertiser* (Adelaide): 12.5.1930, p.15

Chapter 5
61 Musket: *The Sydney Mail*, 20.8.1930, p.32
62 Harry Telford: *The Referee*, 3.9.1930 p.1
63 Jim Pike: *Daily Telegraph*, 26.3.1936, p.31
64 CJ Graves: *The Arrow*, 10.10.1930, p.1
66–7 Tommy Woodcock: Jan Wositzky, *Tommy Woodcock 1905–1985*; Greenhouse Publications, Melbourne 1986, p.33
68 Harry Telford: *Daily Pictorial*, 16.10.1930, p.20
71–2 *The Arrow*: 24.10.1930, p.1

The Shooting: Warning or Spectacle?
77–8 *Sydney Truth*, 2.11.1930, p2
78–9 *The Argus*, 3.11.1930, p3
79 *The Age*, 3.11.1930, p7
83–4 *The Bloodstock Breeders Review*, London, 1932

Chapter 6
85 *The Australasian*: 1.11.1930, p.16
86 Harry Telford: *Daily Pictorial*, 3.11.1930, p.2
87–8 A.B. Paterson: *The Sydney Sportsman*, 4.11.1930, p.6
89 Jim Pike: *Daily Telegraph*, 26.3.1936, p.31
90–1 Denzel Batchelor: *Days without Sunset*; Eyre & Spotiswoode, London, 1949
93 W.J. Stewart McKay: *The Evolution of the Endurance, Speed and Staying Power of the Racehorse*; Hutchinson & Co. Publishers Limited, London, 1933, p.194

Chapter 7
102 Veritas: *The Referee*, 13.4.1932, p.3
102–3 A.B. Paterson: *The Sydney Mail*, 25.2.1931, p.36
104–5 Jim Pike: *Daily Telegraph*, 27.3.1936, p.31

Chapter 8

109–10 Tommy Woodcock: *Sporting Globe* 22.11.1983, p.32 (originally published in
       Sporting Globe in 1936)

110   Tommy Woodcock: ibid, p.33

112   Musket: *The Sydney Mail*, 14.10.1931, p.36

115   Tommy Woodcock: Jan Wositzky, *Tommy Woodcock 1905–1985*; Greenhouse
       Publications, Melbourne 1986, p.44

116–17 Jim Pike: *Daily Telegraph*, 27.3.1936, p.31

118–19 Chiron: *The Australasian*, 7.11.1931, p.15

120   Veritas: *The Referee*, 18.5.1932, p 3

123   David Davis: *The Australasian*, 12.12.1931, p.21

124–5 Bill Stutt: interview with the authors, January 2000

126   JF Dexter: *The Referee*, 17.2.1932, p.1

Chapter 9

128–9 *The Australasian*: 5.3.1932, p.16

129   *Daily Racing Form*: reprinted in *The Referee*, 16.3.1932, p.9

130–1 Snowy Baker: *The Referee*, 2.3.1932, p.11

133   Bert Wolfe ('Cardigan'): *The Herald* (Melbourne), 29.10.1960, p.21

134   Tommy Woodcock: Jan Wositzky, *Tommy Woodcock 1905–1985*; Greenhouse
       Publications, Melbourne 1986, p.53

134   Billy Elliott: *The Sun*, 27.3.1932

134–5 *The Lexington Thoroughbred Record*: reprinted in *The Referee*, 27.4.1932, p.8

135   Tommy Woodcock: Jan Wositzky, *Tommy Woodcock 1905–1985*; Greenhouse
       Publications, Melbourne 1986, p.54

135–6 RE Leighninger: reprinted in *The Referee*, 11.5.1932, p.9

136   Johnny Longden: *The Sydney Morning Herald*, 23.9.1950, p.10

136   David Davis, *The Sun*, 21.3.1932, p.2

Who Killed Phar Lap?

142   Bert Wolfe ('Cardigan'): *The Herald* (Melbourne), 6.4.1932, p.1

144   *The Sydney Morning Herald*, 8.4.1932, p.9

144   ibid

146   Bill Stutt: Interview with the authors, January 2000

148   *The Sydney Morning Herald*, 15.4.1932, p.9

148   ibid

149   *The Sydney Morning Herald*, 28.4.1932, p.9

149–52 *Smith's Weekly* (Sydney), 27.4.1935, p.16

156–8 Dr John van Veenendaal: letter to the authors, 1 March 2000

Epilogue

160   Phar Lap, Unlimited: *The Sydney Mail*, 14.10.1931, p.35

161–2 You ought to have seen Phar Lap: A.B. Paterson, *Off Down the Track, Racing
       and Other Yarns*; Angus & Robertson Publishers, Sydney, 1986

163–4 What might have been: *The Sydney Mail*, 13.4.1932

By Night Raid out of Entreaty

169 Peter Willott: 'An Introduction to the Thoroughbred', in Ross du Bourg, *The Australian and New Zealand Thoroughbred (3rd Ed)*; Penguin Books, Melbourne, 1991

170 Chiron: *The Australasian*, 16.4.1932, p.18

171 W.J. Stewart McKay: *The Evolution of the Endurance, Speed and Staying Power of the Racehorse*; Hutchinson & Co. Publishers Limited, London, 1933, p111–112

172 ibid, p.298–300

174 Chiron: *The Australasian*, 16.4.1932, p.18